Sitting
DUCK

· ·

Published by TechnologyPress, Orlando, FL.

TechnologyPress is a registered trademark.

Printed in the United States of America.

ISBN: 978-0-9983690-8-2
LCCN: 2017907805

This publication is designed to provide accurate and authoritative information with regard to the subject matter covered. It is sold with the understanding that the publisher is not engaged in rendering legal, accounting, or other professional advice. If legal advice or other expert assistance is required, the services of a competent professional should be sought. The opinions expressed by the authors in this book are not endorsed by TechnologyPress and are the sole responsibility of the author rendering the opinion.

Most TechnologyPress titles are available at special quantity discounts for bulk purchases for sales promotions, premiums, fundraising, and educational use. Special versions or book excerpts can also be created to fit specific needs.

For more information, please write:
TechnologyPress
520 N. Orlando Ave, #2
Winter Park, FL 32789
or call 1.877.261.4930

Sitting DUCK

TechnologyPress
Winter Park, Florida

CONTENTS

CHAPTER 16
HOW TO CONTROL AND SECURE BYOD DEMAND

FOREWORD

Television really isn't my thing. If you rule out the college football season and *Curb Your Enthusiasm* re-runs, I barely watch it at all anymore. But I am extremely grateful for TV, because it was one particular show that changed the trajectory of my life. Forever.

In my former life, I was an IT guy. (If you are not familiar with that term, it means "nerd.") I had a network integration firm, now much more appropriately called a managed service provider (MSP). I loved that business. After a day of running coaxial cable, installing token ring network interface cards and rebuilding File Allocation Tables (if you are not familiar with those terms, they mean "big nerd"), I would head home, spend time with my wife and kids, and if CSI was on, turn on the tube.

I don't recall if it was the fifth, fifteenth, or maybe it was the very first episode - I am not sure which one did it - but I do distinctly remember the feeling. That magical episode blew me away. Does crime like this happen in real life? Can technology really be used to catch criminals? Can computers stop a crime from ever happening in the first place? Sure enough, the answers to all these questions was a resounding yes.

I know, because the next morning I launched my own computer forensics company. I wanted to join the fight against crime and evil in our world. And a fight it was. I saw small businesses, where the owners devoted their lives to growing it, wiped out with a few keystrokes. I saw employees quit their jobs and walk out the door with their coat under their arms and the company's data in their pocket. I saw bank accounts emptied by criminals halfway around the world in half a second. In less than three years, my company was acquired by a Fortune 500 who was joining the fight and wanted our skills and knowledge to protect large public companies.

But what about your company? What about private businesses? What about entrepreneurs? Who is going to protect you? In fact, far more small businesses are victimized by cyber-crime than large companies, but who is going to defend you?

These guys will. The guys (guys and gals) who wrote this book. They are, by any definition, heroes.

I believe in small business – what you do – more than anything. I have devoted my life to support and educate business owners. As I travel the globe meeting tens of thousands of entrepreneurs every year, I am constantly humbled by the back-breaking hard work that you do. I am proud of how you support our economy. While I am fighting like hell to serve you, my friends who wrote this book are fighting like hell to protect you. They are the good guys in the fight, and are about to give you more than a chance to protect yourself, they are going to show you every single step you must take to ensure you are never a victim.

You have devoted your life to building your business. I strongly encourage you to now devote the next few hours to protecting it. Turn the page and let's begin.

Mike Michalowicz
– Author of *Profit First*, *The Pumpkin Plan* and other business cult classics and proud nerd for his entire life.

CHAPTER 1

WHY SMALL BUSINESSES ARE A CYBERCRIMINALS #1 TARGET

BY LOWELL BOWDLE

Have you ever been in a situation where your senses perceived danger? Your heart rate increases, and it becomes more difficult to breathe. You become significantly more alert and tense and try to stay calm as the hair on the back of your neck stands up. This intense reaction is your fight-or-flight response from your brain. The stimulus could be thud of a door, or wind blowing through the trees, or noticing something amiss on your computer. Then you realize the cause; you just became a victim of cybercrime but didn't even know until it was too late.

Cyberattacks, cyber-breaches, and cybercrime are on the rise, and small businesses are prime targets. Technology is a necessity in today's competitive business environment, connecting our businesses to anyone, anywhere. Continuing advancements in technology provide increased efficiency and profitability for businesses. Unfortunately, these benefits also enable cybercriminals to have direct access to each of us and our businesses, from anywhere in the world. This chapter will discuss details about why, and how, small businesses are victimized by hackers and what you need to do to prepare for cyberattacks in order to avoid the feelings of helplessness, frustration, and anger, which accompany becoming a victim of cybercrime.

WHAT IS A SMALL BUSINESS?

A small business is an independently owned and operated company, limited in size and revenue, depending upon their industry. The company structure can be sole proprietorship, partnership, or corporation. The U.S. Small Business Administration (SBA) sets standards, according to number of employees and total annual receipts, to determine if a company qualifies as a small business.

If you own, or are employed by a small business, then you will definitely want to read and digest this chapter. If you are a medium or large enterprise company that does not have these protections in place, or has small business partners, then this chapter still contains valuable reading for you.

What should small business owners do to defend against hackers who indiscriminately choose their victims? One great strategy is to learn from other business owners' mistakes, which is exactly what we are going to do in the remaining pages of this chapter. We will explore the three pervasive threats to you and your business and steps you can take to protect your business from these threats.

WHY ARE SMALL BUSINESSES TARGETS?

The first reason is limited investments on necessary technologies. Large businesses allocate much larger sums of capital toward more advanced technologies and the people specifically dedicated to configure, maintain, and monitor those systems. This makes the return on investment much lower for the enterprising cybercriminal who desires an easy living. Why spend all that effort on a company that has layers of protection and monitoring when you can bully someone smaller who has much weaker defenses?

The second reason small businesses are targets is because many business owners believe their company is too small to be targeted – as they do not store important data and their business is not worthy enough to target them. This lack of awareness leads to poor decisions regarding strategies for reducing business risk to data loss. Many of these business owners learn the hard way and begin investing in security prevention after they've been compromised and experienced a data-loss event. Here's the reality; if your data is important to you, then it is valuable to the cybercriminal. If your valuable data were compromised by a cybercriminal, would you consider paying them to regain access to your data? Most likely you would, and this is why your data is as valuable to the cybercriminals as it is to you.

The third reason cybercriminals target small businesses is many small businesses perform services and are trading partners with larger businesses. Since the cybercriminal can more easily find and exploit vulnerabilities with smaller companies, they can then leverage those breaches as a secret conduit or Trojan horse into the larger companies' systems.

The fourth reason why small businesses are targets is many business owners defer business risk decisions to IT and simply wash their hands of any involvement. Cybersecurity cannot be left exclusively to the technology domain. In January of 2017, a study by Boston Consulting Group (BCG) discovered that more than 70% of breaches exploit non-technical vulnerabilities. Your strategy must consist of people, culture, process, and the technical domain.

The following paragraphs highlight the most common and, certainly, the most egregious forms of cybercrime small businesses face: phishing, social engineering, and ransomware. I will offer solid suggestions on what you can do to improve your odds against becoming a victim of cybercrime.

PHISHING

Phishing tactics are distributed broadly through spam emails, as Mary discovered the hard way. These tactics direct you to websites designed to look identical to a legitimate company's website, one you would trust. This is an attempt to deceive you into providing your personal information, such as account numbers, account passwords, address, phone numbers, date of birth, PINs, credit card numbers, and even your social security number.

Mary was concerned when she received an email from Chase about a nonsufficient funds (NSF) payment. As the accounting person in charge of invoice remittance to their vendors, she knew the owner would not be happy about this mistake. She quickly clicked the link and submitted a request to transfer funds from a reserve account to the primary operating account, in an effort to quickly resolve the problem before the owner was notified. This spoofed email mimicked a trusted company, Chase. There is typically a sense of urgency associated with the phishing attempt, such as past due notice, which is intended to distract you from noticing the redirected link. In Mary's case it was the NSF notice.

As Mary took a deep breath, she was satisfied that she avoided this mistake and went on with her day. Well, her anxiety spiked again later that afternoon when she went to reconcile the operating account and noticed transfers from the reserve account to a different bank account. How could that have happened? This could not be happening! The fear and dread of explaining this to the owner was so overwhelming that Mary broke down sitting at her desk.

To avoid phishing attempts like Mary encountered, various methods can be put in place. Implementing an email gateway to filter and quarantine many of these phishing attempts is one example of phishing avoidance. Another method is to hover your mouse over a link before clicking on it. If it is a phishing attempt, the URL will include a link to redirect you to an unknown site. In addition, a legitimate company will never email asking you for confidential information. As a precautionary step, call the company where the account in question is serviced or login to your account directly through a web browser, without using the link contained within the email.

SOCIAL ENGINEERING

Cybercriminals are using publicly available business data, including finding out the identities of executives, financial officers, and senior managers from your website and social networks such as LinkedIn, to successfully launch targeted, social engineering attacks. Social engineering is the act of conning someone into parting with something they shouldn't, such as a piece of sensitive data or transferring money outside the business, as Tim discovered. The mechanism to deliver the attack can be email, fax, or phone.

Tim was the Controller and knew that Robert, the CEO of the manufacturing company Tim worked for, was out of the office visiting customers. Tim returned from lunch and listened to a voicemail message that said it was from the CEO. It sounded like Robert, at least Tim thought it did. However, there was too much back-ground noise to clearly recognize the voice. Tim performed the tasks as he was instructed. He prepared a wire and transferred the funds, as requested, to deal with an overbilling to a disgruntled customer that Robert would explain further after his return to the office. In this case, a criminal posing as the CEO called and left a convincing enough message that Tim did not second guess the request. The instructions were clear enough that he did not need to gather any additional information. You may be thinking, "That would never happen to me!" Unfortunately, it is far more common than you would expect. I know of multiple companies which fell victim to crafty cybercriminals using targeted attacks.

Training your staff to maintain a healthy sense of skepticism, sticking to predefined processes and procedures, and contacting appropriate parties to verify details and ask questions, is the key to becoming a victim of social engineering attacks. The best method to avoid wire fraud is to include a live voice acknowledgement of all wire details, prior to processing the transfer. This one step will eliminate your chance of becoming a victim.

RANSOMWARE

Ransomware is a form of malware that targets both human and technical weaknesses in organizations and individual networks, in an effort to deny the availability of critical data and systems. Ransomware is frequently delivered through spear phishing e-mails to staff members, as Julie and Mark discovered early one morning.

Julie and Mark shared IT responsibilities for a general contractor. At 8:30 one Thursday morning, the helpdesk lit up like a Christmas tree. No one could access any of the files in the file shares and some people couldn't access files on their PCs. An expensive and disruptive nightmare was just starting for this company. The troubleshooting steps resulted in everyone powering off their PCs and laptops until they could access the damage of this outbreak. During that 60-minute window, the ransomware had propagated through their network and the business ceased to function. Not only were the file shares encrypted, but several systems were also infected.

Then, a notice was received from the cybercriminal who demanded payment of a ransom in Bitcoin, in exchange for the procurement of the decryption key, as a means to regain access to their critical business data. As a last-ditch effort, Mark decides to go to their USB attached hard drive where their backups are stored and restore the files from backup. Guess what? The backup files were also encrypted. They were forced into paying the ransom. After that horrific experience, Julie, Mark and the entire management team started taking cybersecurity far more seriously.

When it comes to ransomware, there are three key areas of focus: prevention, business continuity, and remediation. As ransomware techniques continue to evolve and become more sophisticated, even with the most robust prevention controls in place, there is no guarantee against exploitation. This makes contingency and remediation planning crucial to business recovery and continuity.

KEY PREVENTION ACTIONS

- Conduct frequent cyber-security awareness and training programs: Because everyone is targeted daily, all staff members should be made aware of the threats of phishing, social engineering, and ransomware; how these threats are delivered, and how they can be avoided. Through an awareness program, you can actually modify the human behaviors that lead to improved security.
- Implement a cloud or on-site email gateway for more secure email filtering: Since phishing, social engineering, and ransomware can be delivered via email, it is imperative that an email gateway is implemented and maintained. Take much of the complexity out of protecting against malicious email attacks and ensuring confidential information remains secure with a reliable email gateway.
- Apply Patches Regularly: Patches are released by software and hardware vendors with the aim to address vulnerabilities that create security weakness, corrupt critical system data or cause system instabilities. This includes operating systems, applications, and firmware on devices. This can more easily be managed through a centralized patch management system. A consistent process and frequency are imperative to reducing your business risks to these vulnerabilities.
- Remove old, and ineffective, file based anti-virus and malware scanners: These systems are obsolete. Invest in the

next generation endpoint and server protection. To protect your business, you need advanced, signature-less prevention, with behavior based detection and machine learning. It is also important to have policy driven mitigation, remediation, and detailed forensics.

- Manage the use of privileged accounts: Implement the principle of least privilege: users should not be assigned administrative access unless absolutely needed. Those with a need for administrator accounts should only use them when necessary. This applies to local user accounts as well as domain user accounts.

- Configure access controls with least privilege in mind: This includes file, directory, and network share permissions. If a user only needs to read specific files, they should not have write access to those files, directories, or shares. This is especially important in regard to the access allowed to your most important data, which has the highest organizational value.

- Be cautious in what you download: Carelessly downloading e-mail attachments can circumvent even the most vigilant endpoint protection software. Never open an e-mail attachment from someone you don't know, and be wary of forwarded attachments from people you do know. They may have unwittingly advanced malicious code to you.

- Utilize a virtualized environment as the foundation for your computing environment: VMware for example, offers your business the best performance, availability and efficiency from your infrastructure and applications. The improved performance and availability are advantageous as virtual environments allow you to recreate or restore your IT infrastructure, if needed, after a data loss or ransomware event.

BUSINESS CONTINUITY ACTIONS

Since you will rarely know in advance that you are about to experience business disruption due to human error, malicious software, equipment failure, or cybercriminals, it is imperative that you have at least two key components of a recovery plan in place today. As in right now!

- Implement a reliable hybrid backup that includes a local repository with offsite replication. It is essential that you protect your business data from malicious activity, human error and IT disasters. You must have a process in place to verify the integrity of your backups, which includes test restores of files, folders and entire systems. The test restore intervals can fluctuate based upon your business, but file and folder restores would be conducted and documented monthly. You also must ensure the backup logs are checked daily to quickly address malfunctions and errors that occur on occasion.
- Secure your backups. Ensure backups reside on isolated storage, which is physically different from your production storage systems and are not connected to the computers and networks they are backing up. For example, secure backups are stored in the cloud as well as physically stored on premises. Some instances of ransomware have the capability to lock cloud-based backups when systems continuously back up in real time, also known as persistent synchronization. Backups are critical in the event that you become a victim of ransomware as they may be the best and only way to recover your critical data, without paying a ransom.

CONCLUDING THOUGHTS

While the cyber threats to small businesses are immense, the damages do not have to be devastating. By utilizing your good sense, and learning from others, you can take action to prevent your business from becoming a victim of cybercrime and mitigate the effects of these insidious attacks.

About Lowell

Lowell Bowdle is a well-liked and respected consultant with over twenty years of experience in the IT industry, including time as the Founder and President of Assurance Group, Inc. since 2004. Mr. Bowdle has excelled in helping organizations improve their service delivery strategies, cyber security priorities and budgeting decisions, thus increasing the productive time each staff member can contribute to the company mission. The increased availability and efficiencies provide a boost to profitability while also reducing business risks.

Private and public organizations ranging in size from $10 million to over $3 billion in annual revenue continue to leverage this insightful advice to achieve their desired outcomes. Mr. Bowdle is known for being direct, detailed and fact-oriented; clients appreciate the focus on results and accountability where finger pointing and excuses are not permitted.

Mr. Bowdle and his team at Assurance Group, Inc. have a purpose of helping their clients improve their lives and businesses through planning, communicating and delivering relevant advice and the desired results. Mr. Bowdle is actively involved in day-to-day operations where he provides oversight to their managed services and is directly pledged in many consulting engagements with their respected clients.

Mr. Bowdle is the author of an informative monthly newsletter, *The Credible*, which discusses interesting personal, business and technology topics and has a growing readership. He is also a contributor to other trade association publications.

Away from work and client obligations, Mr. Bowdle enjoys spending time with his family at home and outdoors, and attending his kids after-school activities. He has two other passions that he holds dear to his heart and to which he is committed to providing resources each year. Those are research for finding a cure for childhood and adult cancer as well as helping families fight hunger.

Mr. Bowdle and his wife, Shannon, reside in Dublin, Ohio. They have four children.

You can connect with Lowell at:
- Twitter @LowellBowdle
- LinkedIn /LowellBowdle
- Facebook/AssuranceGroupServices
- https://www.assurancegroupservices.com

[Visit https://www.assurancegroupservices.com for a prevention checklist.]

CHAPTER 2

PUT YOUR BUSINESS ON OFFENSE AND NEVER PAY A RANSOM

BY GREG HANNA
– President and CEO of TOSS C³

ran•som•ware |'ransəm,we(ə)r/ *(noun):* a type of malicious software designed to encrypt or block access to a computer system or files until a sum of money is paid.

Our high-tech world has created high-tech criminals. As a result, businesses need to actively engage in proactive measures to stop cyber-intruders from holding their data hostage. Ransomware is a serious problem, having a big negative impact on all businesses. Cybercriminals lock down your systems and force you to pay to unlock them, often stealing your data in the process. For the industrious criminal, they can be paid twice! First by extorting money from you in order to free-up your systems, and then, by selling your siphoned data on the dark web, profiting once again.

If you're thinking, "this isn't a huge risk" or "I've got it covered," don't be overconfident. By not taking deliberate steps to protect your business, you are leaving your company exposed. It doesn't matter whether you use a Windows PC, Mac, Linux, iPad, an iPhone, or an Android, there's a risk. A cybercriminal is waiting for their golden opportunity to hold your data hostage and demand a ransom.

Understanding how ransomware infects a business and what it does will help you devise the best defense against it.

Ransomware can:

- Prevent you from accessing your operating system, leaving your business' information inaccessible
- Encrypt your local system and network files so you can't access them at all
- Infect your computer just by your passing the mouse over an infected webpage
- Stop apps from running, impacting your clients' experiences with your business
- Automatically download itself to computers after visiting a malicious website or one that has been hacked
- Entice a user to open an infected email
- Hide while you unknowingly copy its malicious code from an infected website to your PC's clipboard, and then infect your computer
- Hide malicious code in seemingly innocent pictures
- Hide as a macro in a document
- Demand payment from you so you can regain access to your information using Bitcoin. Bitcoin is a nearly untraceable transaction that almost ensures the criminal gets away with their crime

These malicious activities will rapidly have a negative impact on your business. They stop a company and its employees from functioning during business hours, and compromise clients' data. Ransomware can be a nightmare. To make matters worse, you may pay a ransom and still not get your data back.

It's easy to think that ransomware won't happen to you, but you need to be vigilant and take appropriate action. Your business depends on it. Did you know that according to CNN, $209 million was paid out by businesses in ransomware in just the first quarter of 2016? Criminals have every reason to be motivated and persistent, which is why there are well over two-hundred variants of ransomware. Knowing that cyber criminals won't stop, where do you start?

A RANSOMWARE SCENARIO

Spotting the suspicious, uncharacteristic behaviors of your technology can help you spot a ransomware risk.

You're at work and ready to begin your day. You open your PC, and then things get interesting. Accidentally, you allow ransomware to be downloaded via one of two primary means:

- Drive-by-download: an attack that occurs when a visitor browses a website that injects malware into the victim's PC. These attacks self-execute and run in the background, invisible to the user. This means that the user does not need to take any conscious "action steps" to initiate the attack. It just happens.
- Spear phishing: is a targeted scam with the sole purpose of obtaining unauthorized access to known sensitive data from an identified target. Unlike phishing scams, which cast broad, scatter-shot attacks, spear phishing zeros in on a specific group or organization. The "phisherman" knowingly wants your data, devises an attack, and makes you their unintentional accomplice.

Within seconds, your system is broadcasting malware to the other computers on your network. You have a real problem on your hands and the infection is spreading. Your local files and all network-attached, shared files have been encrypted. Newer strains, such as VirRansom, for example, utilize both ransomware and parasitic virus features. These types of invasions are particularly insidious and nearly impossible for a business to effectively manage. There are no second chances. You must be proactive.

About a year ago, I received a call from a panicked CFO who we'll call Benny. His sixty-user firm was completely shut down. Ransomware had encrypted all files on the servers and PC's. He was frantic and obviously worried.

Our senior engineering team and I got started on the problem. We had to find out what we were dealing with, exactly. During our evaluation, we learned a couple of things:

1. The company had a backup system that was highly inadequate for their needs.
2. The inadequate security software installed required an updated signature file.

The employee who introduced the ransomware into the system had simply clicked on an email link—multiple times. The repetitive clicking lead to encryption on top of encryption because the malware didn't error check that it had already been executed and installed. To fix this problem *as quickly as possible* took *eighty engineer hours*, from Friday afternoon until Monday morning at 4 AM. Only then could we be certain that all the ransomware had been eradicated.

Everything that happened to Benny's firm that day could have been avoided if…

1. The company had a properly functioning backup system that was tested regularly.
2. The staff was properly educated and trained to detect the potential of malware.

Depending upon the type of business, a severe cyber event such as a ransomware infection may lead to significant financial loss, damage of reputation, and potentially force a business to close its doors.

What price are you willing to pay to avoid a ransomware problem?

EVALUATING YOUR OPTIONS

If the thought of paying a criminal money to return your data is unsettling, you need to look towards preventive measures to ensure you're protected.

The average ransom cost is $300.00. However, an alarmingly high number of ransom demands are $1,000.00+. Last year, a California hospital was forced to pay $17,000.00 to free their data after they were spear phished. Most recently, the Los Angeles Valley College paid $28,000 to get their data unencrypted.

So, should you pay a ransom?

To be direct—no! Paying a ransom encourages criminal behavior. These criminals are masterful networkers who will share their lists of targets who are "sitting ducks." Once a victim is identified for paying a ransom, other criminals will specifically target those same people to extort additional money. Adding insult to injury, it is even possible that you may pay the same hacker again, since you've established a history of paying a ransom. How do they flag you specifically? Your company's IP address is like a street address on the internet. Since the cyber criminals "know where you live" after you pay a ransom, they know how to find you again.

You should choose a "better option," one that provides prevention and protection against these costly crimes. Have you ever considered using the services of an IT company that understands how malicious cybercriminals think, and are better prepared to take on the battle more efficiently than most business are?

SAY "NO" TO RANSOMWARE AND "YES" TO THESE 12 STRATEGIES

The best defense against cybercriminals comes from having the right IT partner to help implement security procedures at your business.

With the ever-changing world of technology, consistent attention to each detail about who is doing what on your system is critical—both internally and externally. It's an intensive task, one that many companies cannot master without the help of a professional.

1. **Have regular cybersecurity education and reinforcement training for your organization.** Insufficient or nonexistent cybersecurity training is the largest weak spot in businesses today. Setting guidelines and expectations of how any technology that is used on-site for employees, is necessary. This especially includes any personal devices they may use on your network.

2. **Have your security team (or IT vendor) perform vulnerability and penetration testing on a regular basis.** Taking steps to understand your business's weaknesses must be done so you can put a plan-of-action in place to address them. This testing is frequently outsourced. The resulting next steps necessary to bridge the security gaps identified are either managed by the internal IT department or delegated to the outside IT vendor. A second opinion from an outside third party often uncovers the flaws in current systems, policies, and procedures.

3. **Implement purpose-built technology with zero-day detection, web-filtering, anti-spyware, intrusion prevention, and modern endpoint anti-virus systems.** System hackers work tirelessly, which is why there are so many independent software vendors who are working

frantically to counteract them. The technology vendor TOSS C3 partners with and understands all nuances of cybercrime prevention. This technology can ensure that employees only have access to information necessary to perform their job. This, in turn, isolates any risk to that specific user. Isolation is very effective in preventing and stopping a malicious attack from spreading throughout an entire company.

Another key feature of the technology is its departure from solely relying on blacklists, whitelists and signature files. It is designed specifically to protect your computers and servers from ransomware and other types of malware variations that are known, unknown, and may have only just been released.

4. **Install a quality backup system with snapshot capabilities.** The type of backup system you choose is dependent upon your budget and the type of business you run. The more frequently usable data is backed up, the more quickly you can recover after an event. The question to consider: how much data and time are you willing to lose?

5. **Create a partnership with a third party Managed Security Service Provider (MSSP).** A reputable MSSP can keep your company safe, your data secure, and your reputation intact. You have much to gain from this relationship and much to lose if you choose not to have it. Cyber-attacks can lead to irreparable damage to a company. Your cyber security needs 24/7 attention, which means having an IT partner who can constantly analyze terabytes of log data. When something critical pops up, it needs to be addressed immediately. Most companies who attempt managing this task on their own meet challenges. Often, they just don't have the capacity to monitor the risks and threats, and then fix them.

6. **Put all your IT in the cloud.** Cloud platforms are far more robust and secure than a business network. They use

economies of scale to invest heavily in security, redundancy, and failover systems, which means one thing for a business— you are far less likely to go offline. Threats are constantly monitored and features such as two-factor authentication protect your company from lost passwords, easy passwords, and hacked accounts.

Additionally, cloud companies have many clusters of firewalls, IDS and IPS systems, a Security Operations Center (SOC), and use Security Information and Event Management (SEIM) technology to create actionable items from terabytes of security log data. Cybersecurity is easier to manage and more effective through the cloud.

7. **Keep clear inventories of all digital assets and their locations.** This often lessens the risk of a breach happening that you are unaware of. Begin setting up proper file and folder structure, group policies, and managing access rights.

8. **Avoid downloading files or programs that may be from untrustworthy sources.** Malware authors often use messaging intended to persuade users to perform a download that contains malicious software. A good rule of thumb to remember is if you weren't looking for it, don't download it.

9. **Keep software, operating systems, and applications up to date.** Patching (which fixes security flaws and gaps) can be a pain to do, but it is critical in your defense against system infiltrators. Most IT staff can handle this, which sounds nice, right? It would be if it wasn't usually the last thing on their extensive to-do list. They may update the servers; unfortunately, that's not enough to keep you completely safe. When we conduct our security assessments for clients this is the biggest weak point on the report. The problem with not making certain that routers, firewalls, and computers are patched, is that it gives a malicious party an "in" to your system. Hackers know all the flaws and exploit them.

10. **Segment your network.** No one should have access to more data and resources on a business network than what's necessary to perform their job. Segmentation can prevent a malicious attack that stems through a single computer on a particular segment from spreading to other segments of the network. In other words, the entire company does not have to be breached or impacted. It should be noted that this is a compliance standard for many types of industries, and it is a must for any wireless network to keep production secure from "guests."

11. **Develop a communication strategy to inform employees if a malware attack reaches the company network.** Ideally, you'll have your network segmented and automatically quarantine and isolate any infected computer(s); however, this isn't always the case. Make sure you notify everyone who can be affected—employees and clients alike. Use the intranet, text messaging, emails, or a business continuity provider to get the messaging out. Your goal is to move into action quickly and find a way to broadcast the event and action steps necessary to minimize the problem, while also helping to isolate the incident.

12. **Block file attachments with extensions of EXE and ZIP in email.** This is an old standard practice and one that hackers love to see not implemented in today's world. These extensions make you vulnerable and you should block them or deny them. If your gateway/firewall can filter files by extension, you may also want to deny emails sent with these file extensions.

SUMMING IT UP

It's time to take action. Do not allow a cyber-criminal to disrupt your business.

There is a dramatic and disruptive shift in the IT security industry attempting to turn the tables on the hackers. The security industry has historically lead from behind, reacting to the latest hack and then releasing the fix. Recently, technology has been developed that predicts, observes, and adapts to the attacking code. The best-managed security practices are built on this type of technology, which should bring you hope, as your company's custodian, that protecting your businesses is possible.

When it comes to cyber-security in the 21st century, some of the best advances are not from the trusted "pioneers" of the IT security industry. New companies with fresh eyes and minds are developing the antidote for the cyber-poison that has yet to be conceived.

About Greg

Greg Hanna is an entrepreneur, speaker, best-selling author, and seasoned business executive. Leveraging over 30 years of industry experience, Greg helps CEO's, Presidents, and owners apply the appropriate blend of security, reliability, performance and savings to their IT system, enabling them to achieve their critical business initiatives. Greg has a long history of identifying, developing and launching leading edge technology services, years ahead of industry adoption.

Greg is currently the President and CEO of TOSS Corporation, the IT industry's most in-demand cybersecurity and cloud computing company specializing in highly effective technology strategies bringing true efficiency, agility, and increased productivity to U.S. based businesses.

He is a graduate of the University of Rochester. His business passion is helping companies get out of the technology business by providing them with his IT as a Utility® platform, which is an enterprise-class cloud-delivered IT system complete with provisioning portal, cybersecurity, and 24/7 service and support. Greg's customer service philosophy is, "If each client feels like they are the only TOSS client, we're succeeding."

Greg is the author of *Computers Should Just Work!* and a Best-Selling Author for *Easy Prey*. He has been featured in many publications including the *National Law Journal, Journal of Investment Compliance, Cybercrime: Current Perspectives*, and has been a featured speaker at numerous ALA, ILTA, MGMA, and other Legal, Healthcare and IT events and conferences.

You can find Greg at:
- Greg.Hanna@TOSS.net
- www.Twitter.com/GregHannaCEO
- www.linkedin.com/in/GregHannaCEO

CHAPTER 3

THE #1 THREAT TO YOUR NETWORK: UNTRAINED STAFF

BY JUAN CARLOS BOSACOMA & HERNAN SILVA

It's natural for businesses to want to give access to vast amounts of information to potential clients. However, this also means that you are giving that same information to criminals that are interested in what you can do for them.

For your business, your data is everything. Protecting it is should be a main priority. Doing this is every bit as important as your marketing efforts, branding, and professional excellence. Where many businesses fall short is in ensuring that one of their greatest assets—their employees—are properly trained on how to handle the technology they use on a daily basis.

Do you know what can happen when employees do not know how to use their technology properly? In summary, costly errors that can lead to closed doors, damaged reputations, and hefty fines due to your business falling out of compliance with Acts such as Health Insurance Portability and Accountability Act (HIPAA) and Sarbanes–Oxley Act (SOX).

There are solutions to stop all staff (including management and ownership) from risking their business's data to a cybercriminal's devious behavior.

Employees who work with assets are at particular risk of being targeted by cybercriminals because what they have is of great value to a criminal. They have data, access to monies, and most often very demanding, busy schedules. Without specific policies and procedures in place, it takes just one wrong click to open up a Pandora's Box that is hard to isolate and shut down quickly. The only way to stop a possible breach is to understand the clearly-defined cyber security rules and actively engage in practicing them. As IT professionals who have an engaged focus on employee training, we know that all the technologies and safeguards we put in place are less effective when employees do not understand the significance of their actions with the technology they rely on.

You need only ask one question: do you know if your business has its bases covered? Are your employees "fool proof" against criminals that want your data and resources for their own gain?

COMMON WAYS THAT CYBERCRIMINALS TARGET FIRMS LIKE YOURS

Cybercriminals take the time to know your company well, and find the weakest spots. That is where they will get their "in".

Cybercriminals are master researchers. In a short amount of time they can find out the names and emails of Managing Partners, CFOs, CEOs, and other key influencers and decision makers. Likewise, they can find out the names of those people who handle company assets, such as monies or confidential, critical information. And once they do, the trouble can begin.

We want to share two common scenarios with you to help you understand the craftiness of these cybercriminals. They are very smart and determined individuals and groups of people who choose not to use their intelligence for good.

Scenario #1 – phishing

Bookkeepers and accountants have access to the money in most organizations. This makes them an ideal choice for a cybercriminal to target. With the information they've learned about your company, they will create an email that looks like it's coming from a person of authority. In many cases, it may be a very normal request—one that doesn't make the employee think twice. They want to do their work efficiently and certainly not "waste" management's time. The request that morning is for a wire transfer for $45,000.00 for a new account for a business transaction. The money is wired and then there's no thought about it until…the transfer is inquired upon. But by the time that happens, it is too late. The chances of ever getting that money back again are likely gone. It was an unintentional employee error that could have been prevented with the right rules and policies in place.

Scenario #2 – ransomware

You're a law clerk and an email comes in with a new attachment, stating that it's information for one of the attorneys about a new case. The clerk opens it up and in an instant, a virus is sent across the network. Everything is frozen up and all business halts. The link was a virus and the sender of it may want money in exchange for giving you access to your data back, or they may just want the confidential data that your system holds. Again, the employee had no ill intention with opening the link. They just didn't know because the right training hadn't been offered.

These scenarios are frightening and real. They can happen to the CEO just as easily as the Receptionist if the proper training isn't in place. If you are ready to make sure your employees are equipped to protect your business assets, you need to take action today.

ELEVEN WAYS TO EDUCATE EMPLOYEES ON CYBER - PROTECTION

It is through a committed team effort that businesses can ensure all employees are trained and knowledgeable on all aspects of cybersecurity on their technologies.

The efforts that are involved to ensure that all employees are up-to-speed on their roles in protecting the company's assets from cyber-attacks, is a joint effort between IT and user-awareness. When the guidelines we are sharing with you are adhered to, your risk of being hacked and having your business interrupted are reduced significantly, if not nearly completely. Employees are no longer the weakest link to your data, because they are trained and alert to the warning signs.

1. **Keep a clean machine.**
   Never save anything that should not be on your computer that is not imperative to your work function. This will reduce the risk of malware and viruses entering your system via that document or image. Additionally, you should never leave a work document open on your desktop when you are not there working on it. This will eliminate that "passerby" from stealing critical data of a client, or even on you. Login lock your desktop when you leave your station.

2. **Use good password practices.**
   Depending on the type of business you operate, all passwords should be changed a minimum of quarterly, but monthly is even better. In general, the longer the password the better. It should include special characters, numbers, and letters (uppercase and lowercase). Passwords should also:
   - Never be used twice
   - Be unique for every site or application used
   - Use two-factor authentication, which means that one of the verifications goes beyond just a user name and password

An important function of the services we offer at CIO Landing is to help ensure that the proper password protocols are being met by applying system policies and training.

3. Clean desk policy.

This involves your physical desk and making sure that anything you have on it is not vulnerable to a thief. You should never have your passwords on sticky notes on the side of your computer, or even in your desk drawer. Make sure that you don't leave documents with Personally Identifiable Information (PII) exposed so anyone who passes by can view it.

4. Evaluate all incoming correspondence.

When a new email shows up in your inbox, take a few moments to evaluate it for validity. As much as software can analyze for spam mail, at times some can get through because new ways to disguise it are constantly being initiated. These emails can contain malicious links, online ads with malware, and even messages from friends that have tricky subject lines such as "thought you might like this." Employees should be trained to:

- Glance at an email and see signs that it may be harmful
- Have a clear understanding of who to go to if there is a problem
- Be willing to ask if they are unsure before opening email content

You have to know how to look for the clues. One of the most unique services CIO Landing offers is testing to ensure that employees really are following the guidelines put in place for safe use of their technology. On occasion, we send out test emails that look and feel like they might be legitimate, but the signs that they are not are also present. If the employee clicks on a link, for example, they'll get a friendly reminder to not do that. Then, reports of how these continuous training efforts go are reported to the proper management. They're not designed to be "got you" moments, because even upper management can find themselves on that list. These tests reinforce training and show how effective it is, or is not, once an employee is done with face-to-face training and back in their work environment.

5. **Share the risks that you learn about.**
Alerting office staff and personnel about what you've noticed as potential risks is a great way to give everyone a head's up of what they may encounter, as well as to put a "real life situation" reminder out there for them to be aware of.

6. **Be aware of what is safe to plug into your computer.**
USB sticks, in particular, need to be paid attention to. If you receive one in the mail, make sure you can identify the source. A common scheme cybercriminals do today is to toss a USB with a well-known company name on the ground in the parking lot. Someone sees it and picks it up, they get curious and plug it in, and then they instantly discover that malicious activity is taking place on their computer, or their entire system is jammed. Some criminals like to cause mischief, nothing more.

7. **Set guidelines for using mobile devices for company purposes.**
When an employee can link to a company's website, software, or system from their mobile device, certain things must be done to ensure protection, including:
   - Have a way to lock and monitor the device remotely
   - Ensuring that the ability to remotely wipe the device exists
   - Encrypt all corporate data on the device

8. **Training on how to not fall victim to social engineering.**
Imagine sitting at your desk and you get a call from someone. They identify who they are and state that they're with your IT company. They ask if your computer's been running a bit

slow. You mention that it has and then they tell you to go to a website and perform a test. You do, and then—BAM—you're hacked.

Or, someone walks into your business wearing a shirt with your IT company's logo on it. They introduce themselves as new to the company and say they need to do maintenance on your main server. You take them back to the server and don't think much about it. They gladly follow, of course, and then they plug into your server and steal the content from it that they wish to possess. This can happen and it's bold, because so many people somehow imagine cybercriminals being little rats in the dark, but they can be some of the most charming, well mannered, and lovely people you'll ever encounter. Take a few moments to look up the name Olga Komova. She's a woman that could have been a model, but chose to be a multi-million-dollar cybercriminal instead. She fooled people for a long time.

Your business must use smart practices and confirm identities of new IT people for the firms they work with. We can assure you, that when we hire someone at CIO Landing, we introduce them personally to the clients so they get to know them. You shouldn't expect anything less than that. It's not only good business to have that expectation, it's also smart business.

9. Email security.

Any firm that sends and receives confidential or classified information (which is all firms) must have email security in place. Secure email is encrypted. Period. The best technologies for encryption should be used, and there is no excuse to not do this step.

10. Physical security.

Criminals will break into businesses in the dark of the night when they are looking for something of value. Don't give them easier access to anything. USB drives should always be in protected areas, computers should be shut down for the evening or password protected and paperwork that has confidential data on it should never be exposed. This physical security is the common sense that helps a business be protected even if someone should steal actual computers, or even a server. Your IT services company should be able to set up the ability to disable these devices as soon as you realize what has happened. It will significantly reduce the damage that can be done as a result.

11. **Data protection, retention, and destruction.**
   It's easy to want to keep every record or document your business has forever, but if it is not a necessary document, destroying it properly is your smartest choice. How we store data has changed over the years, but its disposal must be done properly. Take CD ROMs, for example. They seem obsolete in many ways today, but that doesn't mean you just toss them in the trash when you're done with them. You need to shred them. If you donate computers, wipe them clean. Have a well-defined policy in place for your business on how the disposal of obsolete property and information is to be performed.

These common sense tips offer businesses good assurances that they are taking the practical steps to ensure that the information and assets their company is entrusted with are secure. Businesses who do this are the businesses who earn clients trust and maintain longer lasting, fruitful relationships.

A CENTRAL SOURCE FOR REFERENCE

Training your staff to protect your business is one of the best investments you can make. It's a benefit in all areas of peoples' lives, because technology is here to stay.

It's exciting and wonderful to live in a world where we have access to so much information. However, technology also brings a serious responsibility to be aware of the threats that come with having access to these vast amounts of information. This is why having rules in place, as well as an Acceptable Use Policy (AUP) for your staff members, will help your business to thrive.

An AUP lays out the rules, policies, and procedures that show you've invested in staff education on cyber security, and it also gives their acknowledgement that they are willing to comply by the guidelines set. This is all necessary for business, and with the help of a sound IT partner, it becomes more manageable. The time has come to ensure that you are as secure as you must be. Take proven, actionable steps and throw away the speculation.

About Juan Carlos

Juan Carlos Bosacoma, Founder and CEO of CIO Landing is responsible for the company's strategy, sales and marketing. He is continuously focused on ensuring their clients are delighted with their services. CIO Landing clients have the peace of mind that comes from knowing they have the business-technology partner they need to run their businesses. Juan Carlos is a Microsoft Certified Professional Specialist (MCPS), Microsoft Certified Networking Professional Specialist (MCNPS) and Microsoft Small Business Specialist (MSBS), Certified HIPAA Security Professional and VMware VSP among others He has 30 years of IT industry experience and the expertise to provide their clients with the highest-quality technology solutions.

JC worked for several large companies including CAP Gemini, Time and Quaker Oats developing software and applying technologies and processes to improve performance and profitability. JC started his first company, USHost.com, in 1995 – one of the first Internet Service Providers in Chicago. After selling USHost.com in 2002, JC founded CIO Landing to provide small and medium-size businesses with the technology previously only available to Fortune 500 companies.

Born in Bolivia, South America, JC received a scholarship to attend the University of Buffalo where he received a B.A. in Computer Science, and completed graduate work in Industrial Engineering and Computer Science. He later attended the University of Chicago where he received his MBA.

In his time away from the office, JC enjoys paddle tennis, soccer and playing with his two children. He particularly enjoys his family, friends and good food. He is also a member of the Chicago CEO Roundtable, Illinois Hispanic Chamber of Commerce and University of Chicago Investment Club, and is an ex-officio Honorary Vice-Council of Bolivia.

JC can be reached at:
- jc@CIOLanding.com
- https://www.linkedin.com/in/jcbosacoma/

About Hernan

Hernan Silva is the Vice President, Engineering Operations at CIO Landing. He received his B.A. in Business Administration from Northeastern University as well as numerous technical certifications, among them: Microsoft Certified Systems Engineer (MCSE) Servers, Microsoft Certified Professional (MCP), Cisco CCNA, A+, MIT Honor Code Certificate for Cybersecurity, Evolve Academy for Cyber Security Training, CompTiA Security+, Certified HIPAA Security Professional, Clio Certification, Scrum Fundamentals, VMware VTSP, GS10K.

Hernan has worked for small and large companies throughout his technical and entrepreneurial career. These include Micro-Tech, USA, Dell, Uwins and White Paper Computacion in Argentina. In 2005, he formed USA IT Help, a successful Managed Service Provider company based in Chicago which merged with CIO Landing.

Hernan is known by clients as someone that will solve any and all technical problems while making sure clients become raving fans of the company.

CHAPTER 4

I'VE BEEN HACKED! WHAT SHOULD I DO?

BY SCOTT SPIRO
– CEO of Computer Solutions Group, Inc.

Collaborative efforts between businesses and qualified entities that can help prevent cybercrime are a necessary function for business in today's world.

There are few illegal activities on the rise as rapidly as cybercrime is. According to *Key findings from the Global State of Information Security® Survey 2017,* which was conducted by PricewaterhouseCoopers, there was a 38% increase in the instances of phishing scams and other cyber-security incidents. These breaches are not isolated to computer systems alone, either. Today's cybercriminal will also hack cloud architecture and now mobile devices. In fact, 28%+ of the incidents in the survey were on mobile technology. Ultimately, these are the reasons why 55% of individuals, businesses, and other entities now collaborate with cybersecurity specialists to better ensure their safety.

Defending yourself against these criminals is nearly impossible to do alone, especially if you rely on any technology to conduct your business, or you like how technology enhances your personal experiences in life. It's a high-tech crime by professionals that is hard to counteract with amateur efforts.

Significant strides have been taken toward effective prevention of breaches and the disruption that ensues from one. Depending on the intent of the hacker, a business may have their data stolen, which is most assuredly a compliance concern, particularly in the medical and financial fields. However, every business of every size is vulnerable, because there is one thing that you have that criminals want—your data. They are willing to work relentlessly, 24/7, using technology that tries to find the weakness in your technology's security.

As a business owner or decision maker, the steps you take after you discover you've been hacked are critical.

Some breaches are immediately detectable. Ransomware is the best-known example of this type of breach. This crime involves file encryption and then there is a demand for ransom that follows—pay the ransom and they will decrypt your files and release your information back to you. If the ransom isn't paid in time, you may lose your files completely. An additional concern that is not uncommon is that you may pay ransom, but still not get the files back.

Other breaches are slow and use spyware, making it so you don't realize they've been stealing your business data for a long time. Most businesses notice in 200 days, according to the FBI in LA. In addition to this, there is an estimated $4.6 million per month stolen from cybercrime.

It can be challenging to grasp the severity of a security breach, but it is a crime—always. The one thing you do not want to do is assume your business won't be victim to one. The odds are against you, and the threat is serious enough that the federal government has even released guidelines to help you recover from an attack.

THE FIRST CRITICAL STEPS TO TAKE AFTER A HACK

Urgent: (of action or an event) done or arranged in response to a pressing or critical situation.

You've been hacked. Don't dwell on it, or think a computer reboot will solve your problems. This is wasted, valuable time. Even if your breach took place a month ago, what you do from the moment you're aware of a breach, matters greatly.

1. **Stop using every device that is infected.**
   If you are not certain which devices are impacted, stop using all of them until you can connect with your IT service provider. Connect with them immediately, as well, because communication with them is imperative from this point on. Ideally your IT partnership will already have the right systems in place for helping to determine which devices— both on your business's site and through BYOD or COPE plans—are infected.

2. **Notify relevant parties of breach.**
   Getting the word out that your business has been compromised is necessary. This requires letting all employees know, alerting potentially-impacted clients, and also contacting any media outlets or federal entities that require you to report the hack for your specific business.

3. **Reset all passwords.**
   The new "norm" for passwords is to change them periodically for routine maintenance and enhanced security. This is logical with the 10 million user password hacks that occur daily. However, Microsoft has recently changed their password security recommendations to be even stronger, but these recommendations do veer in a different direction from what people have become accustomed to hearing about. As an authority in the matter, they do feel these recommendations offer more solid protection to users. These steps include:
   • Maintain 8 characters—longer is not necessary

- Eliminate the character composition requirements
- Eliminate the mandatory password change requirement
- Ban common words to keep vulnerable passwords out of the system
- Educate your users regarding not reusing their password for non-network related purposes
- Force registration for multi-factor authentication

4. Begin a forensics evaluation.
This is imperative. Start by asking: what was the reason that someone wanted to gain access to the system? Was it for intellectual property, client data, etc.? Your business was targeted and it is important to know why, exactly. This information is highly valuable to federal cybercrime divisions such as what are in the FBI, IRS, and Department of Homeland Security. If there is a trend showing on the vertical (similar businesses) more can be done to pinpoint, identify, and hopefully prevent your business from being attacked again. Plus, similar businesses can take proactive steps to not become the next target. This type of cooperative teamwork is how local and federal authorities can work together to help businesses and make cybercriminals' jobs much more difficult.

It should also be noted that hiring the qualified examiners necessary to do a thorough, full-forensics investigation is highly costly. You will save considerable amounts of money by proactively investing in the technology and user training to help ward off cyber-attacks from infiltrating your business. Plus, you'll save on reputation and potential fines and penalties. Basically, working backwards is always costlier than moving forward in a secure manner.

5. Perform an updated virus scan on your entire system.
Most major tech companies will have ways to get your account back up and running and with minimal data loss if you invested in the proper backup system technologies.

However, this can all be in vain if you don't remove every single virus that may be on the system. Failure to remove all threats can mean that you could restore your systems one day and have to begin all over again the next.

6. Determine the need for credit monitoring.

Whether the hack was on you personally, or a business hack in which they were able to retrieve large amounts of Personally Private Information (PPI), you will want to have credit monitoring in place for impacted victims. Identity theft is a serious crime, and according to the 2017 Identity Fraud Study released by Javelin Strategy & Research, $16 billion was stolen from 15.4 million US consumers in 2016, compared with $15.3 billion and 13.1 million victims a year earlier. In the past six years, identity thieves have stolen over $107 billion. These numbers show why criminals are incentivized to gain access to your data.

7. Remain in communication, as deemed necessary.

Communication is critical after a hack between the IT provider, impacted business, and the appropriate authorities. The communication required includes:
  i. affected businesses coming forth with any and all things they recognize is not operating properly;
  ii. the IT company explaining what they are doing, and why, while also giving guidance to smarter practices;
  iii. the IT company and business both communicating with authorities, as needed, to help them gain the valuable data and information that can help them solve cybercrimes.

These efforts help keep all parties informed, as necessary, and lead to better documentation of all actions and outcomes during a highly stressful time for a business.

Once you take action after a hack, you can hope to return to normal business practices with minimal impact via lost records and downtime. However, it is estimated that 60% of all small-to-mid-sized businesses that are breached do go out of business within one year. Being proactive and not taking your technology's security for granted will help you prevent becoming a statistic.

SMART SOLUTIONS TO PREVENT DISRUPTIVE CYBER EVENTS

Businesses have more control over maintaining their business assets and data than they often realize.

Businesses should embrace the active role they can take in ensuring that they do not become the victim of an attack. There are many things that can be done, proper technology aside, which will help strengthen their defense and ward off an attempted breach:

1. **All employees must be trained.**
   You can have the most sophisticated technology in place to protect your business system(s) from a breach, but if your employees do not understand their role, any system you may have is rendered less effective. Think about a security system for your home. We put it in place to protect our loved ones and our possessions from a criminal entering into our home. If that criminal comes knocking and your kid answers, the entire security system that is in place has just been bypassed. The same is true of your business, and the way in which your employees adhere to security guidelines and safe practices.

2. **Teach employees about the various ways that criminals gain access to information.**
   Social engineering is a way of tricking employees to give a criminal access to certain targeted information. This crime can either take place through email correspondence, or in some cases, through bold criminals who will walk into a business pretending to be a "new employee" of a service your business already uses. You need procedures in place

for verification and identification.

An effective way to ensure that employees are always engaged in safe practices is to do training exercises. We have this type of testing available at Computer Solution Group in which we send out test emails to see if we can collect personal information or company data. Then we collect the results that show how often employees clicked-through and track it for training purposes. More often than not, the targets for email scams are going to be those who have access to funds and information a criminal wants. This makes CEOs and other C-level folks prime targets.

3. **Be diligent in ensuring your technology is as protected as possible.**
   Patch updates and systems checks are necessary functions of any IT department that your business employs. There should never be delays to getting these updates done, because in those gaps there is a great potential for a breach.

When it comes to your business's technology as a whole, having a partnership with an outside IT firm is the best way to ensure that everything that should be done is getting done. When companies such as Computer Solutions Group come in as an outsider, we can look at the entire system and see where it is strong and where it is weak. As with most things, your technology is only as strong as your weakest link. Regardless of whether it is untrained employees or lackluster technology, it can be corrected.

UNITING AGAINST THE CRIMINALS

All cybercrime prevention for businesses is a joint effort of sound leadership within the organization and the vested interest of the employees.

Through gaining the cooperation of the leadership and decision makers, you can create unity within an organization so everyone recognizes why they should be on board with newly- implemented policies and procedures to do their jobs in today's world. This adaptation is certainly easier than the alternatives, which include:

1). a business that can no longer sustain after a breach
2). employees having to seek new employment
3). personal peril from the risk of stolen PPI

One of the largest benefits CSG brings to our clients is that we also work in partnership with the FBI, as well as the Department of Homeland Security's Cybercrime Task Force. Through these collaborative efforts, we are able to learn about what's trending in cybercrime, as well as offer data and insights as to what's happening in our market, which serves the Greater LA area.

These are the steps that will better empower us to all work together to help manage businesses more smartly, as well as to create a more aware culture that is highly unfriendly to cybercriminals.

About Scott

Scott Spiro is founder and CEO of Computer Solutions Group Inc., a two-time *Inc. 5000* Honoree, and author of the Amazon Top 10 Best Seller, *The Business Owner's Guide to IT and All Things Digital*, as well as a sought-after speaker.

In addition to solving the typical I.T. challenges most businesses face, Scott has focused his own efforts in helping his clients and their families battle Cybercrime, Cyberbullying, and other harmful technologies. A member of the U.S. Secret Service Electronic Crimes Task Force, Scott is dedicated to protecting both businesses and consumers from the potential dangers of being "connected" 24/7 to their computers. Additionally, with two small children of his own and some recent health issues, Scott began development of a new program designed to help business owners better manage their technology and lifestyle. This sometimes means turning it all off in order to focus on not just their businesses, but also their health and loved ones.

A graduate of UCLA, Scott had originally planned to go into the Entertainment field. However, a knack for technology and an interest in entrepreneurship led him along a different path.

Scott has appeared on the *CBS Evening News* with Scott Pelley, *KTLA Channel 5 Los Angeles*, *KCAL 9 Los Angeles*, *NY Times*, *Los Angeles Times*, and many other publications.

CHAPTER 5

FIRST LINE OF DEFENSE

BY JASON SILVERGLATE

The notion of a "first line of defense" is a simple, yet inherently complex structure, vital to any business's IT systems. The first line of defense can be broken down into *five components,* **DNS, Firewall, Network topology, Desktop** and **Security Training,** to form a multi-tiered defense to protect your data and your business. Each of these components provides valuable protection from the ever-increasing threats posed to your business by increasingly sophisticated and relentless cyber criminals.

These criminals will attempt to attack your business in every way possible. Tactics in their constantly growing arsenal include: sending your employees or clients phishing emails, exposing vulnerabilities in your firewall or router, infecting websites your users visit, and leveraging insecurities in the applications you are running. With all these tactics looming in the cyber world, one main question looms ahead of your business. How do you protect your business, and your livelihood, against these unyielding threats?

First Component of a First Line of Defense: **DNS**

One significant way to protect your business is to create and maintain a strong, comprehensive first line of defense. The first component to this first line of defense is a Domain Name Server, more commonly known as a DNS. By utilizing a secure DNS platform, you are essentially creating a shield around your entire network. This protects your business in several ways. First, a DNS platform can weed out, in real time, malicious websites users might inadvertently visit. Second, it helps prevent an infected computer from communicating with a ransomware server, interrupting the encryption process and preventing your data from being held hostage. A secure DNS platform provides real time insight into which users are doing what and provides the ability to filter the websites and services your employees are able to visit.

Let's play out an all too common scenario. An employee receives an email and clicks on an attachment to track a FedEx package. Unfortunately, the email was a phishing email, so by clicking on the link your employee just inadvertently downloaded and installed the ransomware payload onto their computer AND your business network. Guess what? If your business does not have a secure DNS platform in place, you've just been hacked. That is all it takes for cyber criminals to get inside your network, inside your business. If your business does utilize a DNS Platform, then you are protected. The payload will not be able to communicate with its control server to trigger the encryption, because the servers would be blocked. This component of a first tier of defense does a great job catching the low level, tricky attacks before they can even get into your network and can cause real problems. This is great protection, but a secure DNS is not perfect, and working alone, it will not provide enough protection.

Second Component of a First Line of Defense: *UTM Firewall*

A firewall is the next component necessary to create a strong line of defense. Most businesses run legacy basic firewalls, which only provide basic scanning of traffic flowing into the network, and then allow all traffic from within the network to flow out. This poses huge security risks and opens the network up to multi-attack vectors. Running a modern firewall, specifically a modern UTM Firewall, is critical in providing an overall, multi-faceted defense against a variety of actions an attacker might take. UTM stands for Unified Threat Management, which allows for a variety of security-related applications and infrastructure components to be managed and installed on a single device.

Most modern UTMs consist of the following: Gateway Anti-Virus, Gateway Anti-Malware, IDS (intrusion detection), IDP (intrusion prevention), Anti-Spam, web-filtering and VPN. Putting this type of UTM Firewall in place is a lynch pin in any comprehensive defense strategy. It will scan every bit of data coming in and out of your network and every bit of data going from one VLAN segment to another, if properly configured. A proper UTM Firewall will constantly scan and analyze to make sure your data is not infected or compromised in any way. A basic firewall makes no sense in today's threat-filled cyber world, for any type of business. For protection that truly makes an impact, all business must use a UTM firewall.

Third Component of a First Line of Defense: **_Network Topology_**

95% of businesses I talk to fail to implement the simplest of all the defense layers, Network Topology. This missing piece of a first line of defense strategy is a major reason for many of the infections and security breaches those businesses experience. Implementing a great firewall and secured DNS are worthwhile efforts, but can only do so much on their own. Segregation of your networks into logical VLAN's (Virtual Local Area Networks), which is what implementing Network Topology entails, allows your UTM Firewall and DNS to do even more. Each function in your business should have its own VLAN: your servers, desktops, Wi-Fi, and guest Wi-Fi. For example, your manufacturing desktops and your office desktops should each have their own separate VLAN. This will force all traffic between the network segments to go through the UTM Firewall first, where it will get scanned and analyzed for malicious payloads. This allows a virus, malware, or ransomware to be stopped before it reaches all aspects of your business network.

Consider this scenario, an employee brings in a USB stick from home and plugs it into their computer at work. Unbeknownst to them, the USB is infected with a virus. If you do not have proper Network Topology in place, that virus can run rampant through your entire business network and infect your core servers, crippling your business for days or even weeks. If your networks are properly segmented with Network Topology, that virus will hit your UTM firewall and be disabled before it even has the chance to permeate through the other segments of your business network. Implementing Network Topology is a no-brainer.

Fourth Component of your First Line of Defense: **Desktop**

This final component of a comprehensive first line of defense is your Desktop and its corresponding Anti-Virus/Anti-Malware programs. Unfortunately, no matter what Anti-Virus or Anti-Malware program you use, these types of programs have become the least effective means of preventing real problems within your business. Despite the fact that these programs offer the least effective protection, they are still a crucial part of strong, multi-tiered defense. Relying solely on your antivirus and antimalware is a critical mistake most business make, but in today's cyber-threat landscape it is simply a mistake no business can afford to make. A solution is to upgrade to modern *Next Generation Endpoint Protection* (NGEP), the next evolution with a radically different approach to antivirus and antimalware.

An important feature to look for in an NGEP is the ability to learn the local systems and environment so the NGEP will not flag benign behavior. A NGEP should also share immunization across the entire network, enabling protection from an infection on one machine to all machines in the network. The new protections included with NGEP firewalls are infinitely better than traditional antivirus and antimalware, but are still only effective when used with the other components of a comprehensive first line of defense.

Fifth Component of your First Line of Defense: **<u>Security Training</u>**

Unfortunately, the weakest link in a security defense is the human element. This means a business's own employees are the single biggest cause of infection in an office environment. Most often, their intentions are innocent or unintentional, but by clicking on attachments in emails, visiting malicious websites (generally unknown to be malicious), taking their laptops on the road, connecting to insecure Wi-Fi access points, and bringing in infected USB keys from home or elsewhere, employees play a direct role in infecting business networks. As an employer, you really cannot blame them. They simply just don't know any better.

This is where your opportunity to protect your business lies. By utilizing online training services and in-office seminars provided by your MSP (Managed Service Provider) you can educate your employees and empower them to help protect your business instead of unknowingly sabotaging it. Educating your employees at least once a year, or even better, quarterly, on how to be safe and secure when using technology, is an absolute necessity into today's threat-filled landscape.

THE IMPORTANCE OF MULTI-TIERED DEFENSE LAYERING

Let's take a look at a typical business's infrastructure, one that hasn't implemented a multi-tiered defense layer. This type of business will have an undersized firewall doing only inbound "port-filtering", a basic firewall function, and antivirus software on their desktops. Does this sound like your business? If so, this a pretty simple setup that can be breached and abused in numerous different ways.

Consider another business. This business has a secure DNS system in place. The business has a correctly-sized firewall scanning all traffic across their VLAN segments, all inbound and outbound traffic. It also utilizes proper VLAN segmentation, isolating each segment from one another, protecting it from infection from the other segments. The business also has implemented NGEP on all desktops and servers. Every quarter, the business provides cyber-security training to all employees.

Which business do you think can survive an attack and come out on the other side of it? Hopefully, it is obvious to you that the second business can survive the attack and come out with no, or very little, negative effects. The first business does not stand a chance.

There is no getting away from the fact that the threats in today's cyber world are immense, constantly increasing in quantity, extent of damaging effects, and sophistication. This does not have to mean your business must experience these negative effects of cybercrime first hand. Take action today to create a strong first line of defense for your business, and you can drastically improve your business's defense against becoming a victim of cybercrime.

By implementing the five strategies discussed in this chapter, *DNS, Firewall, Network Topology, Desktop and Security Training*, your business will experience a drastically stronger defense against cybercriminals.

About Jason

Jason Silverglate is the co-founder and Chief Executive Officer of Continuous Networks — the most trusted leader in IT Support for NY / NJ since 1997. An innovative executive, he thrives on building something from nothing and finding creative solutions to complex problems, whether it be technology or business related.

Passion is what drives Jason in all aspects of his life; passion for life in general, technology, simplicity, and the chase. He surrounds himself with people who are equally passionate and share his goals and values. Some of these people include Jason's beautiful wife Allison, his dedicated business partner Ross, and his amazing team who demonstrate their dedication to their customers and success daily.

Jason got his first "computer" in 1984 from his parents. This sparked Jason's interest in computers prompting him to start a web design company at the age of 16. Jason attended Rutgers University, graduating with a double major in Computer Science and Finance. By the age of 19, his web design business changed into "DedicatedNOW" the predecessor of Continuous Networks and has been growing since then. Jason is always looking for and learning about emerging technologies, keeping his pulse on the industry—continuously!

Jason is a serial entrepreneur with a passion for technology and business. He sets the bar high for himself as well as for his teams and loves to see results in hours/days in contrast to months and even years!

As a former volunteer fireman, Jason likes to be prepared for anything. His wife says he work too much. It's possible...

Contact Jason at:
- Jason@continuous.net
- 973-572-1066

CHAPTER 6

THE #1 WAY CYBERCRIMINALS HACK INTO YOUR NETWORK

BY WAYNE SPRINGER
– President and Owner of Atiwa Computing, Inc.

In a world filled with choices, the decision to take steps to prevent your business from being hacked is a no-brainer.

It's impossible to overstate the risk to businesses that exists if they've been hacked. Just a single occurrence of being a victim of a cybercrime is often enough to shut your business down for good. All those years of work and dedication, gone. Employees displaced; reputation lost. This does not have to happen, because there is a great deal that can be done to understand how cybercriminals think, and create defenses that deter them from targeting your business.

Cybercriminals have an advanced strategy to gain entry into your systems, and they know when you are not prepared to defend yourself.

Years ago, people only had to worry about annoying spyware and malware on their computer systems, but the world has changed. Over the past five years, the game of hacking found an opportunity in ransomware, in specific, Cryptolocker. Once criminals realized that they could encrypt a business's data and hold it hostage until they were paid a certain amount of money, it was game on. They were excited! This is why ransomware is one of the easiest sources of revenue a criminal can hope for. There is no risk to them and they are given an opportunity to rob people on a mass level.

Today, cybercrime is an actual industry that has a structure, including a business model to follow and conferences to learn how to master the craft of cyber-theft. While I might go to a conference to learn about new and exciting IT technologies, a cybercriminal will attend one to learn how they can become your business's disruptor—your nightmare is their payday.

RANSOMWARE IS A LUCRATIVE BUSINESS, EARNING AN AVERAGE FEE OF $679 PER HACK

Knowing that ransomware is golden, do you know how a hacker picks their victim?

There is one primary way that your system is most vulnerable to a hack. That is email. At current reported statistics, over 58% of ransomware attacks begin with email, either via clicking on a link embedded in the email, or else by the user opening an attachment that is included with the email. These sorts of email are call phishing scams, a criminal practice that sends emails that appear to be from reputable companies or entities with the purpose of gaining access to personal information, including passwords, credit cards, banking information, etc.

The success rate of these crimes is about .4%, which may seem low, but when you break it down, that "low" number tells a different story. Consider this:

If 100,000 people receive a malicious email about 400 will *get hit. About 40% of that 400 will pay the ransom, which means there are 160 paying customers—a/k/a victims! In this accurate scenario, the bad guys just made $108,000.00 for a few minutes' worth of work. The bad-guys' networks run 24/7.*

Do you see why this is worth their time?

If you are thinking that this is a crime that won't come your way, you're being lulled into the exact position criminals want you to be in—the vulnerable one.

Hacking is a big-time crime, but not just for "big businesses." Today, small-to-midsized businesses are prime targets.

With the quickly-advancing sophistication of cybercrime, the risk has grown even more dangerous. Many small-to-midsized business owners, managing partners, CEOs, and CFOs feel that their business is safe. They may not even see what they have as being of value, but this can be a costly mistake. Because bigger companies were the targets for so long, the smaller businesses feel safe. This is not true for one reason—the security measures are now in place for big business, leaving small and mid-sized businesses as prime targets for a hack. The bad-guys have time for your business, and a desire to disrupt it.

Cybercriminals see these types of businesses as low hanging fruit and response patterns have shown them that these outcomes are inevitable:

- If a business loses its data permanently (intellectual property and client data), they face the possibility of going out of business.
- The fear of going out of business is enough to make most companies eager and willing to pay ransom to get their information back quickly.
- The bad-guys now realize that holding your data ransom is

even more profitable than stealing your data for the purpose of re-selling it to other bad-guys.

Cybercrime has become so advanced and these evil minds are excellent researchers. They can learn so much about your life just by the little clues you leave everywhere. What you post on social media about your personal life can be used to gain access into your business's computer system. For example, if you mention your children's names in a Facebook posting, the bad guys know that people often use their children's names, or variations of their names, as passwords on their computers because they are easy to remember. If the bad guys can discover when you are out of town on vacation, that can alert them that it may be a good time for them to start an attack. The bad guys know exactly who to target, as well. People who are higher up in an organization are most vulnerable. Why? Because they are the ones with the most access to information, are very busy, and often not paying attention to the fine details of what is happening on their computer.

Do you know the one critical mistake most small-to-mid-sized businesses make about their assessment of hackers?

It's not uncommon for people to discredit hackers as some teenager working from their basement or a tech-minded person with no social skills. Nothing could be further from the truth. These criminals are among the smartest people in the tech world. For years, they have been ahead of the curve in recognizing and exploiting weaknesses for their own gain. The main areas of weakness they look to for setting up their crimes are:

- Untrained employees
- A lack of advanced defense-based technology
- Companies that have no other option than to comply with their demands

All that needs to take place to see if your employees and business have weaknesses is to either send an email with a malicious link, or to find that open back door that takes them right into your computer system without you even recognizing it. Once they have your information, they have options.

In addition, we've learned that these sophisticated hackers are now offering their services for a fee or for a cut of the ransom, to other, untrained, unskilled hackers who are simply following a "play-book" of what to do. In this way, the bad guys can expand their reach and grow their businesses exponentially. And of course, unfortunately, there is virtually zero risk, zero downside, to these hackers – since they almost never get discovered or punished for their crimes.

WHERE DOES THE DATA THAT'S NOT HELD RANSOM GO?

Cybercriminals know where to go to learn and improve their game, and also to sell the information they steal. They learn from each other, and partner and collude with each other. There is an entire underground marketplace called the "dark web". This is where bad guys conduct their business. They buy and sell:

- Guns
- Drugs
- Child porn
- Human Trafficking
- Data
- Intellectual property
- Access to systems (pay ransomware once and you'll be targeted again)
- Credit card numbers
- Any and all Personal Private Information (PPI)

We call this the "Cybercrime Iceberg". What we mean by this is that the visible internet that the good guys see is only about 5% of what's out there online. Basically, it's the tip of the iceberg. The dark web is the other 95% of that iceberg. The dark web is home to illegal operations with pornography, guns, stolen data, etc. You can't find it by searching a keyword, either, because it's craftily hidden through long tails and password protected entry that is only give out to criminals who've been vetted as qualified enough and smart enough to be given access.

This is startling, of course, but you can gain an edge by understanding how you're targeted for hacks and then taking steps with an IT professional to help you minimize your risks.

Here are a few different areas in which a business (and individuals) can be vulnerable to a hack attack.

- Password hacking: from all that personal information that people share, which includes kids' names, special dates, and other locations, hackers have software that runs analysis of likely passwords that people may have. It's not so hard to find it, either. Just recently, we had to go in and help a law firm with a recovery and situation where a hacker was demanding $17K in ransomware. They'd entered the system through cracking the receptionist's password. Guess what the password was? *Password*, literally. A startling high number of people actually use the word *password* for their password. Part of our services at Atiwa Computing includes implementing systems that call for passwords to be of a certain strength (a combination of characters, numbers, upper case, and lower case), as well as required password changes every 90 days, perhaps sooner depending on the business. Plus, we recommend having different passwords for different programs. This isolates the risk in a hack.
- Malware and spyware: malware disrupts and damages a computer, and spyware is secretly on a computer watching what the user is doing, where they go on the internet, and even keeping track of keystrokes. This gives access to incredible amounts of information, ultimately, and your habits and interests can be used against you. To lessen this risk, our company uses sophisticated state-of-the-art NGEP (Next Generation Endpoint Protection) technologies

and detection systems, which are constantly running and analyzing risks based upon dynamic rather than static threat detection. What this means is that these new technologies use a form of artificial intelligence to look at the dynamic behavior of a company's network, rather than just trying to compare a potential threat to a static, out-of-date list of known viruses and threats. Based upon any alerted changes in typical behavior, then alarms start going off to let network managers know that a hacking threat has been detected. It's like an early-warning system—the "canary in the coal mine," so to speak.

- Social engineering: using social media and general information available on the internet to create a familiarity factor that leads to the victim trusting the intentions of someone who is really a criminal.

- Drive-by downloads: these are legitimate sites with malicious code. They often take advantage of un-patched software on the end-user's computer. Software manufacturers such as Microsoft usually patch their holes the first Tuesday of each month, which leaves about 30 days of vulnerability that hackers will use. Only severe threats are addressed more often than that. Staying on top of all threats in real time is a way that we help counter this risk for our clients.

- Rootkits: these are software tools that allow someone to gain access to a computer system without being detected. It's like sneaking into a closed office that doesn't contain a security camera or system. The data can be taken unnoticed. This is nearly impossible to be successful at if you have the proper safeguards in place for your business.

- Zombie computers: these are computers that are on the internet which mask as legitimate enterprises. When you are getting emails from places you believe are credible they are actually marking who they are and what they are, preparing to find a way into your computer system or gain valuable data from you.

- Skimmers: these are used with credit cards, which means that you want to be alert if you are a business who uses a credit card swiper. The way a skimmer works is that a small device is put on the card reader that transmits the information on the card to a small computer, which is operated by the criminal. In turn, they sell the credit card number. This is a profitable enterprise! Businesses need to have a procedure in place that is mindful of looking for skimmers so they are not a player in this high-tech crime. Unlike many technology crimes, this one has to have a local presence in order for it to work.

- Downloading "free" software: the problem with free software is that developers do not make free software without getting some type of return to remain in business. Antiviruses may be free, but you have to pay for all the upgrades that really make you feel assured. And while the "free" may be with good intention, hackers know that fixing patches that keep you from being at risk is seldom a priority. This is why you have to be careful if you use free software for accounting, bookkeeping, and other programs that rely on confidential data. You'll also find that you release these companies from any obligations that may occur in the "fine print" on their Terms of Acceptance.

It's hard to grasp devious thoughts and patterns from criminals when most people operate from a mindset that they are doing good business with good people. However, those who are out to get your business are likely not a recognizable face. Because of this, cautionary measures need to be taken.

Our goal at Atiwa Computing is total protection of our clients' valuable data, client information, and files. We want to put all of our clients under a protective "bubble". This process begins with a thoughtful conversation with our clients. We do a thorough, in-depth assessment of their current state in order to evaluate and determine their risks and vulnerabilities.

Through a cyber security assessment, we can determine how vulnerable a business may be, and help find a corrective course of action—before it's too late. Sadly, far too often we're brought in after the crisis takes place and it doesn't make anyone feel better to look in hindsight at what could have been done to prevent this from happening. The "post-mortems" (those done after a hack has already occurred) reveal to us that about 97% of the attacks we've seen could have been prevented, *if* the right tools and processes had been in place beforehand.

Our goal is to prevent businesses from ever paying ransomware, having to report data breaches to authorities, and being the victim of crimes committed by malicious outside parties against their organization. It isn't a tall order to have this goal, as it's very achievable and affordable with the right technologies in place. We are the ones who can put the required technology into place, and into action protecting your business.

> *It's not till the tide goes out that you find out*
> *who's been swimming naked.*
> ~ Warren Buffet

About Wayne

Wayne Springer is the founder and president of Atiwa Computing, Inc., one of Houston, Texas' largest independent computer services companies, and recognized by the *Houston Business Journal* Book of Lists as one of the Top CyberSecurity companies in Houston. Wayne is also the author of the book, *Hassle-Free Computer Support*. Entrepreneur, speaker, and seasoned business leader, Wayne is passionate about helping protect small- and medium-sized businesses from the world's I.T. and cyber-bullies. Wayne and his team enjoy helping to eliminate all the hassle, waste, and headaches of all things digital in people's offices.

A little about Wayne: Prior to founding Atiwa Computing, Wayne held various executive positions with United Energy Resources in Houston, and Fluor Daniel in California.

Wayne also served five years as a U.S. Army officer following his graduation from the United States Military Academy at West Point, New York. In addition, Wayne holds an MBA degree from Southern Methodist University in Dallas, Texas.

Wayne can be reached at:
- wspringer@atiwa.com
- https://www.linkedin.com/in/waynespringer/
- www.Twitter.Com/AtiwaComputing

CHAPTER 7

HIPAA COMPLIANCE: UNDERSTANDING YOUR BUSINESS'S ROLE

BY BILL WHELDEN
– Rx-IT, Founder and CEO

Whether you are a covered entity or business associate, you have to be mindful of HIPAA. Your business depends on it!

Every organization that is associated with the healthcare industry has heard of HIPAA. But do they really know what it is? In short, HIPAA is the Health Insurance Portability and Accountability Act, which was passed in 1996. It's been updated two times since its inception and it does impact you if you are:

1. A covered entity: an organization that provides medical service. This includes doctors, dentists, chiropractors, etc., and also your health plan (your medical insurance company).

2. A business associate: a third party that provides services to a covered entity that comes in contact with peoples' Personally Identifiable Information (PII) or Electronic Personally Identifiable Information (ePII). This might be an accounting firm, attorneys, medical equipment service companies, transcription services, and even an answering service.

We're living in a world where peoples' private information is stored in computer data bases in many locations. This puts them at risk of being exposed to unsavory parties, who either want to gain access to their data for medical identity theft or to sell on the dark web, a place where criminals look for their "in" to devious behavior. HIPAA deals with medical records and information, in specific.

If you are a covered entity or a business associate, you have an obligation to take HIPAA seriously. There's no room to use excuses of "I didn't know" when it comes to protecting patient information. However, the compliance guidelines and expectations are so complex that very few, if any, organizations of any size, can effectively manage HIPAA compliance alone—even when they have a Compliance Department. There are some IT companies that know a lot about HIPAA, and I know that it's one of the busiest, most robust services that the Rx-IT team offers.

THE ILLUSION OF "HAVING IT COVERED"

Reliability and stability in your IT relationship is imperative for HIPAA compliance.

Let me share a story with you. It's a common one that has taken place in many businesses at one point or another, but this particular case is one that I worked on some time ago.

There was a physician's practice whose IT "department" consisted of the fairly tech-savvy boyfriend of one of the receptionists. When they needed something done, they relied on him and he did what he could. Then there was the "break-up" and that practice found out that they were being broken up with too. The "ex" was no longer willing to wear that IT hat. They called my business to get some IT support for computer and software updates, patches, etc. Their systems were running slow and things were getting frustrating (which is often when people finally break down and call IT professionals—when they just can't take it any longer).

When I went into the practice, I began to go computer to computer to find the problems. What I discovered was an abundance of malware on their systems. At one point a cat even ran across the screen encouraging an employee to click on it to get the winning lottery numbers. This explained the slowness of their system and it highlighted their vulnerability. I had to ask, "How do you handle HIPAA Compliance?" The person showing me around casually replied, "One of our doctors does that." When I asked to speak with that doctor I learned that he was on a sabbatical for that year. Hmm… in case you're wondering—this is a very serious problem!

After fixing their computers, giving some necessary advice about not allowing employees to do whatever they wanted on their work computers, and setting up a service plan, I approached HIPAA. I offered some more detailed explanations about the risks that they were exposing themselves to by not heeding the policies and expectations of HIPAA's compliance requirements. To be blunt—they had no idea. And many businesses do not, until it's too late.

Businesses and practices that are obligated to HIPAA compliance don't have room to make mistakes. If they have a data breach, the best-case scenario is that they can receive a fine of $100 per compromised file, and the worst-case scenario is $50,000 per compromised record—and potential jail time. Yes, it's that serious. So, what do you do?

THE SPIRIT OF HIPAA

Your efforts and intentions to be HIPAA compliant are easy to identify if your business should ever be investigated. Likewise, your lack of effort is also easy to spot.

HIPAA is like a moving target, something that is feared and resisted because it is challenging to understand in many ways. For example, you could call HHS (Health and Human Services), which oversees compliance and ask someone questions. They answer, and if you were to call back you'd have a good chance of getting yet another answer. How frustrating! It takes a true commitment to professionalism and knowledge about the topic to ensure you're getting the right answers. Far too few entities realize that qualified IT staff are usually the best qualified to manage that function and all the expectations that come with it.

If you're a covered entity, it's mandated that you have a compliance officer and a privacy officer. More often than not, the compliance person is also the privacy person. If this is your situation, two questions should immediately be pondered:

1. What would you do if that sole source of information was gone?
2. What would happen to your compliance and privacy efforts if that sole person quit?

If you had a HIPAA breach, you would not get a free pass because the one in charge was on vacation, or they had quit and you just hadn't gotten around to training someone else. It's a "no excuses" Act, which is why it should be of high importance to you. If you own your healthcare-related business, staying in business may depend on your level of compliance. Few organizations can afford the hefty fines that come with HIPAA violations.

Doing everything you can to ensure you are protecting your patients' and clients' privacy through HIPAA is how you meet the spirit of HIPAA.

Here are some suggestions that will help you meet the spirit of HIPAA, which, when they are followed and adhered to in their entirety, often lead to great results. Your business is protected, and your patients are too. Because if you have a breach, depending on the complexity of it or what happened, you are required to report it to your local media and the Department of Health & Human Services (HHS). It's no easy task to rebound from that type of bad exposure, which is why it makes sense to embrace what you can do proactively.

It's not my intent to overwhelm you, but I am definitely interested in helping you to understand the severity of your inactivity when it comes to HIPAA compliance and operating within the spirit of it *at all times*. The last place you want to end up is on the Wall of Shame. Have you heard of that?

The Wall of Shame is where your name lies when you've experienced an event that leads to a HIPAA breach of 500 records or more. When breaches of this size happen, you are required to immediately report them to HHS and it immediately becomes public information. Anyone can pull it up at any time and the information remains there forever. In 2009, the HITECH Act was passed and this requires the secretary of HHS to publicly report breaches of protected health information (PHI) affecting 500 or more individuals. On September 26th of that same year, the "Wall of Shame" was born.

As of March 2017, there are a total of 1845 names on this wall. Just recently, a healthcare provider in Indiana got their server hacked and 80,000 records were stolen. Anthem Healthcare, a covered entity, had a breach of 78,800,000 records compromised—that's close to one-quarter of the population of the United States! This is scary stuff, and being a part of those types of statistics is highly damaging. If you are a practice or associate that doesn't have an endless cash flow, you're going to go out of business within a few years of an event where you're breached. Cleaning up the mess with offering the compromised victims credit monitoring for a few years hardly compensates for any challenges they may have as a result. Additionally, some states have even more strict guidelines than HIPAA, and HIPAA was deliberately crafted so that if more restrictive state or local laws are present, those guidelines take precedence.

There are solutions that you can take. This is in your control.

1. <u>Cross-train two employees as your HIPAA compliance officers</u>: This is the best way to have the right attention being paid to HIPAA at all times and you should always have two people trained. Additionally, in life things happen—people take vacation, they get sick, they look for other careers. None of those things should leave you vulnerable in the HIPAA compliance area.

2. <u>New employee training</u>: Before any new employee is able to access your computers or other office technology, make sure they are properly trained in HIPAA. Undertrained employees pose a serious risk.

3. <u>Have all employees attend HIPAA training at least every other year</u>: Compliance guidelines are continuously changing and they don't give you a period of time to adapt to them. Though having training from the proper source whose job is to stay on top of HIPAA guidelines, your business is to maintain the spirit of HIPAA.

4. <u>Document everything</u>: Having policies and procedures in place for everything helps ensure that policies and protocols are followed at all times. This includes:
   - Keeping up with maintenance
   - Password policies
   - Logs and records of maintenance and password updates
   - Document your business associate agreements for all contractors—this is an agreement for people who come into contact with information you trust them with—that states they will follow HIPAA procedures and guidelines. With or without the agreement, they are still liable, but it is a professional way to emphasize your expectations of their compliance for your business. *In addition*, covered entities are required to have these agreements.

5. Have policies for Bring Your Own Device (BYOD) and electronics that are business-owned, but can leave the premises: Tablets, smart phones, iPads, and any other devices that can leave the office *must be encrypted*. If they are not, it's a huge issue and risk. If that device is lost or stolen, it has to be secure so any confidential and privileged information on patients is not compromised.

6. Everyone needs to be aboard the HIPAA train—yes, even doctors—no exceptions: Admittedly, this is the toughest challenge that most medical service providers face. But there cannot be exceptions and waivers to this rule. For example: if a computer or tablet is in an exam room, they must ensure that another patient's information is not showing on that. Leaving it exposed IS a HIPAA violation, and a big deal. The way to conquer this challenge is to understand that HIPAA compliance is like a habit. It may seem inconvenient and it is, but it's essential that the written policies to safeguard your patients' information become second nature to everyone in your practice or company. It will take time to have it come naturally, but every employee needs to be diligent about it.

7. Have a good relationship with your IT vendor: Your IT vendor is your business BFF! They have a significant obligation to your business's wellbeing, and helping you safeguard your patients' information, in specific, is much easier to master when it's in a reliable IT vendor's hands. A good IT provider offers (without exception):
   - The proper updates to software and hardware
   - Record keeping for all electronic parts of your business, including service logs and records
   - The ability to constantly monitor your system for unnatural conditions that could spell trouble
   - A good, sound business plan that ensures your business understands the spirit of HIPAA is evident
   - Training for employees to more easily identify malicious activity on their computer, should it occur (phishing scams, malware, ransomware, etc.)

- Any and all services that help secure and strengthen computer technology, digital data, and ePII
- Annual risk assessments

Are you the Principle, Manager, or responsible party of a healthcare practice or healthcare-related business? Then you are someone who needs to be on top of this. When questions are asked and challenges arise, ultimately people will turn to you. Show them that you've got it covered.

MASTERING HIPAA

Regardless of what size your business is, get help to ensure you are HIPAA compliant.

Whether you have an IT department in place or not, your business should seek out assistance to make sure they are covered when it comes to HIPAA compliance. The most logical way to do this is to seek out an annual external audit—a group of professionals that know all the guidelines for compliance and can view your business with an impartial eye. This more than pays for itself when it comes to taking the right steps and being able to demonstrate that you've operated within the spirit of HIPAA, should a breach occur.

A professional, qualified IT service provider is going to be attuned to your practice and its daily functions. Furthermore, they are able to resolve issues in a timely manner without disrupting your business, particularly during business hours. Their expertise in your business's safety is easily identified; your questions easily answered.

Over the years the world of IT has changed and moves rapidly to keep up with the creativity of malicious parties that wish to sabotage business networks in some way. All businesses are vulnerable, but those that deal with ePII are particularly intriguing targets. That's why the Rx-IT network not only makes sure we stay abreast of all HIPAA guidelines, but also state regulations across the U.S. Technology has become a Return on Investment (ROI). Today it is looked at as an asset, not just an expense, and because of this, those businesses that take IT issues seriously experience fewer problems, higher security, and better business growth and branding.

What type of business do you wish to be?

About Bill

Bill Whelden is the founder and CEO of Rx-IT, a concierge IT service provider for healthcare practices, businesses, schools and non-profit organizations. For nearly two decades, Rx-IT has focused on providing service to its clients that goes far beyond the scope of a traditional IT service provider.

Bill started installing network wiring in offices 25 years ago. In those early days, he learned to build business computers and servers to setup complete, networked business systems. It quickly became apparent to him that frustration and resentment with IT companies was growing because of unexpected system failures, unpredictability of cost and the inability to obtain immediate and competent IT support when it was needed. So, Bill went back to school and earned certifications in the Novell server operating system. Then, after more school and work experience, Bill became a Microsoft Certified Systems Engineer. Later, Bill earned certifications from Comp Tia, Cisco and Sun Micro Systems. As a result, Rx-IT was born and became one of the first technology companies to offer proactive support and fixed pricing.

Today, Rx-IT continues to deliver world-class service, security and hyper-responsive support to its clients. Many of those clients have a history with Rx-IT going back to its early days.

CHAPTER 8

SOX COMPLIANCE: REMOVE FEAR AND GAIN CERTAINTY

BY CHRIS SCHALLEUR
– Partner at Christo IT Services

The compliance and regulatory hurdles that come with running a good business can be conquered with the right resources.

In 2002, Congress passed the Sarbanes-Oxley Act (known as SOX). This Act is designed to protect investors from potential fraud due to unethical accounting activities by any firm (first or third party) that provides a financial service. It mandates that these businesses have a highly-disciplined focus on the financial disclosures they release, and requires them to file quarterly reports with the SEC.

The purpose of SOX, in and of itself, shows its serious nature to any business that must comply with it. We understand the concerns of businesses that take SOX seriously, which is why Christo IT has ensured we are a knowledgeable and effective IT source that can partner with diligent CEOs and CFOs.

When we first meet clients who have SOX compliance concerns

they are often in a state of panic. These concerns and anxieties are logical because it is a huge undertaking to have in place the safeguards and policies that demonstrate you take compliance seriously. We understand this and our goal is to educate and demonstrate how a business can gain the assurance that they have it covered. If SOX were a 'pitch black' sky we would be the beacon on the lighthouse guiding people safely to shore.

WHO'S RESPONSIBLE FOR SOX COMPLIANCE?

It is always easier to take the time to put policies in place than to explain why you didn't take the time, especially to the SEC.

The CFO and/or CEO are ultimately responsible for SOX compliance. They submit quarterly reports to the SEC. These reports are meant to demonstrate that compliance is being met. Their signature is the one accountable for the compliance. It's a big responsibility, which is why coordinated efforts and group cooperation are so important.

For SOX compliance, in specific, the signature means that your organization has adhered to the internal auditing process for that quarter, that all is accurate, and that if a problem is detected you will disclose it quickly, as legally required. If the firm is small enough to not have people in these positions, it doesn't change the expectations of compliance. A solid and reliable expert in SOX compliance needs to be brought in. Christo IT offers this service, and it all begins with an Audit of what is currently in place.

This is a thorough Audit that is done in the spirit of the same seven-page form that SOX requires, should a problem arise. There is no more thorough option. Most customers can agree that filling out this form proactively, instead of after a problem is noted, is preferred!

On this form we walk through the entire technology evaluation process, step-by-step, to discover any flaws in technology or policy that must be addressed. Your smart and compliant business practices are everything when it comes to your integrity and the ability to hold up to any internal or external corruption that may be present. A few of the main points the Audit touches on include:

- Physical security of data and technology
- Encryption of data and information on servers/computers
- Proper training for end-users
- Yearly evaluations and reviews of processes

Review is only effective if it's followed by action. Risks are categorized between green, yellow, and red, with red being the most severe. Then the problems are addressed. What happens when they are ignored? Well, it's not great. That seven-page report that feels overwhelming can suddenly become the thirty-to-fifty-page report. This massive report isn't done by companies like us, your friendly IT partner, either. The SEC steps in and that means you are in an official Audit, with all the intense emotions that come along with it.

IF YOU WEAR THE COMPLIANCE HAT, WHAT CAN YOU DO?

Make sure you create an IT partnership with an organization that excels at SOX compliance.

Few people in leadership positions are underwhelmed. They have a lot to do and many times that means technology gets put on the "I'll-do-it-later" list. In today's high compliance, cyber-threat world, this is no longer feasible. You need to do your due diligence, which means you need IT support. No excuses! The IT company you choose to work with makes a big difference in helping you master what must be done so your business can thrive.

The starting point of this relationship is to perform a baseline audit of your entire technology system, as well as the policies and procedures that are in place for all employees. This is how gaps and risks are exposed and we can see what's missing.

Why do you want to use an outside IT provider for this? That's a question we hear often. The reason you typically want to go external for the Audit is because it offers a neutral set of eyes that can objectively look at the big picture and small details that encompass your business. This is how you can determine processes and a plan to make sure your business is doing what is necessary for SOX compliance, efficiently and effectively. These efforts are also conscious of:

1. Cost Effectiveness: If they cannot be immediately implemented, immediate action should be taken to create a budget for enhancements that are necessary or recommended.
2. Risk: Prioritize what should be done first, according to both the level and the span of risk (red, yellow, green).
3. Business Drive: Technology that helps your business be protected and compliant is technology that must be invested in.

Participating in this shift to security is imperative. If you're a brokerage firm of even ten people, you must do this. It's not just for the "big firms." Businesses that deal with stocks, investments, 401(k)'s, portfolios, etc., need to be SOX compliant.

THE THREE MAIN SECTIONS OF SOX

Your business's detailed reports of your continuing efforts to comply do matter.

The main areas of focus on the technology aspects of SOX lie in (1) the internal controls, (2) evaluation, and (3) disclosure. Together, these make up the whole and help business leadership ensure they're taking the steps required by law.

I. Internal Controls

An external Auditor cannot be the source that is driving results. They must be the evaluator of the policies and procedures that are in place from the business's internal efforts. This includes addressing the following items:

- Acquiring and maintaining software: You can have partnerships with an IT firm for management and updates; however, you must still show that you have the proper reporting and policies in place for your business—and on-site.

- Application control and auditability: Business controls for systems and LOBs (line of business applications) must be in place to monitor who is signing into which applications. For investors, this may be their portfolio system. Lawyers may use a docket system. Accountants will use some sort of tax software system. The following items should be easily viewed:
  - Login attempts and exceptions, including failures, origins, numbers, general, specific or individual user's failures.
  - User controls, which can mean several things: 1) system users only have access to what they need; 2) there is a way to immediately remove anyone from the system who is fired or leaves their position. This is important for isolating compromises and also for securing data from parties that should no longer have access to it; 3) an emergency process that handles crises where an abrupt change of position takes place.

- Acquiring and maintaining infrastructure: Identify each section of the system and assign responsibility. This is an organization chart of the systems that lays out every piece of the business's technology needs and attaches a name to it to show who is responsible for what. This includes servers, LOBs, training security software, vendors, etc.

- Infrastructure resource protection and availability: Testing of the continuity plan is part of this internal control and it is largely determined by the risk assessment that is performed.

Questions such as these are asked: What happens if the trading system goes down for 24 hours? What is the backup plan? What's the "big red button" for the backup plan? What criteria cause this plan to "go into action?" Continuity does lean toward technology, but it is a risk assessment for the entire business, as well. It involves:

- Regular testing, evaluating of processes used, and reviewing reporting on failures and exceptions
- Having processes for resuming standard operating procedures in the event of a compromise or system malfunction
- Monitoring of the entire system to identify all activity on it
- Determining the needs of the system on a regular basis
- Knowing what exceptions are in place (ex: how many log-in attempts can be made before a computer is locked out)

- Infrastructure maintenance: Create and adhere to a baseline for all of a system's needs, from daily to scheduled reviews, all which include adjustments and changes, maintenance, patching, upgrades, risks, vulnerabilities, and security needs. This also includes:
  - Firewalls, switches, and other network hardware
  - File systems, databases, devices, and directories
  - External points: Where is information being transferred? Is there authorization for the activity, proof of transmittal, and proof of receipt?
  - Ongoing training of users, as needed after specific patterns have been discovered, and also as a part of standard procedure
  - Asset reporting that includes date of implementation, dates of review, and dates of retirement
- Maintain changes: When systems are in place, procedures are agreed upon, and people are assigned to specific tasks, you need to begin evaluating when you make changes, who makes them, and why. The process needs to be in place to ensure information is always up to date. For example: if we

are in March 2019 and have a baseline of March 2017, you need to show the changes that have taken place, exactly, over that period of time. You should be able to see each change and understand the change, its necessity, which areas the change impacted, and in what manner. This includes:

- Impact assessment, prioritization, and authorization: Requests for changes need to be assessed to determine what impact they have to systems, to ensure changes in management system are followed, and what the initiative solves (ex: moving the risk from yellow to green), estimated amount of downtime so proper planning can be made. This even includes training time for new software.
- Emergency changes need to be defined and have a process.
- Processes to note change status tracking and reporting must be evaluated to determine if adjustments are made or best practices are being compromised.
- Security testing, vulnerability testing, and penetration testing should be done as necessary or, at a minimum, annually. In many states, they are considering the documenting of this law.

• Install and accredit solutions and changes: Plan and budget ahead to master your technology, rather than scrambling to catch up because a mandate is put in place or, worse yet, you have a SOX compromise. This includes having:

- Test planning in place prior to implementing security changes. This review must analyze the performance metrics for the baseline and reporting.
- A post implementation review that can spot if the process is doing what it's intended to do or what improvements need to be made.

II. Evaluation
Evaluating all the measures taken is the only way you can be assured they are doing what is intended with them. This includes:

- <u>Governance</u>: Which leadership role (CFO/CEO) is in charge, and who has the ability to view what information?
- <u>Measurement</u>: What are we looking for? What events require action?
- <u>Recordkeeping</u>: Where are the processes and policies kept? How are they updated? How are they available, and to whom?

This evaluation stage involves accessing restricted or secure information, which means that you first need to determine which people in the organization should be granted access to it. Typically, it's only management and leadership level positions that can access this information, particularly when it's actionable.

III. Disclosure

You want to have a system in place to save time and sanity for the CEO and CFO. It makes a huge difference! Assuming a business of about fifty people, you can do your mandatory quarterly SEC filing in about eight hours with an effective system in place. Without it, you are looking at a process that could take days or even weeks. In a world of constant obligation, what CEO, CFO, or leader has the time to do this, while also staying on top of their other work obligations? Especially every quarter?

The quarterly disclosures may not be officially audited, but they are signed off on by a CEO or CFO who is taking responsibility for their accuracy. If lackluster efforts and breaches of said policies are found, they will first go to the person who signed the filing. Do you really want to risk it being inaccurate? Imagine what that could cost you as well as the business you have a leadership role in.

WHAT'S YOUR NEXT STEP FOR FINANCIAL DISCLOSURE COMPLIANCE?

Choose to be engaged in SOX compliance.

I admit, it's not fun to talk about such serious topics with businesses, but when you compare it to what happens if you do not, it's worth it. Christo IT has an obligation to educate and serve as many businesses as we can in SOX compliance. The partnerships we create from this play an important role in a business's success and adherence to the guidelines and policies that are in place.

It's through continual engagement in what's taking place that consistency is found and solutions are created. Once a system is in place, it cannot be forgotten about for five or ten years, and then you start all over again. This is not efficient or effective. Being prepared to navigate employee turn-over, emergencies, and other unexpected things that can happen in your business is necessary. Your reputation, as well as your business's existence, depends on it. You should welcome the thought of being the positive headline—the one that is known for protecting your clients and your business's professional integrity.

About Chris

Chris Schalleur founded Christo IT Consulting in 1999, with the goal of providing the type of professional IT support larger companies enjoy to small businesses in the Philadelphia region. Applying his experience working in Marketing and Sales, as well as IT and Engineering at firms such as Honeywell, Primavera, and Microtrac, Chris quickly built a reputation for superior IT Services for Small Business. Chris has been a leader in the Philadelphia region for Small Business IT Services.

With encouragement from Harry Brelsford of SMB Nation and Microsoft, Chris started the Small Business Server (SBS) Philly User Group in 2006. The group is comprised of IT professionals in the Philadelphia region who serve Small Businesses. They are dedicated to improving best practices, learning about new technologies, and increasing customer awareness in the region.

Chris is an Engineering graduate of Villanova University. He has been a Microsoft Certified Systems Engineer since 1998. Chris is a multiyear award winner of the SmartCEO Future 50. With Chris guiding the firm as CEO, Christo IT has also been awarded the Wharton School "Philly 100", given to Philadelphia's 100 fastest-growing companies, for 3 years in a row.

Chris is an award-winning speaker, both locally and nationally. He has won Connectwise IT Nation's "Best Breakout Session" as well as their "Outstanding Software Solution."

Christo IT provides IT services that will allow your business to breathe a sigh of relief knowing that a trusted IT service provider is on your side. Technical glitches happen, yet small businesses in Philadelphia trust in Christo IT's proactive programming. Christo IT encourages you not to let your business fall short of effective PC services that will allow your system to stay current and up-to-date with all of the advanced technologies of today's world. Christo IT is always on the cutting edge with new programming and software, allowing their clients to receive only the best PC services.

What Christo IT wants for all of their customers is 99.9% uptime. The only way they can guarantee that is by providing you with a Complete Care™

Experience — that is, Premier IT consulting services around the clock.

Chris lives in North Wales, PA with his amazing wife, Jen, and his two wonderful daughters, Julia and Emily.

You can connect with Chris at:
- Chris@ChrisIT.com
- www.twitter.com/ChrisIT
- www.linkedin.com/in/chrisschalleur
- http://www.chd2.com

CHAPTER 9

CYBER-BREACHES IN THE MEDICAL INDUSTRY
HOW TO PREVENT BEING THE NEXT STATISTIC

BY MARIA LEVIN

In the medical industry, the risk associated with lackluster security on your network can have costly consequences.

You go to work and are logged onto your computer, catching up on emails. You open up the next message and it has a link, asking you to click on it. You do. You're in a hurry, after all. Afterwards, something strange starts to happen.

On your computer, a small window opens and closes, almost as quickly as the blink of an eye. Then you begin to notice some disk activity. When you go to open some files, the icon has a lock on it. You click on it, anyway, but the file still doesn't open. Instead, a message appears which reads: these files are encrypted. A code must be entered to decrypt them and gain access.

It's startling, and you read on. It turns out that this code will be made available to you when you pay a ransom through bitcoin. They are holding your information hostage.

You think, *what just happened*? What happened was that you were hacked and infected with ransomware.

Ransomware is a type of malware that computers in the medical and dental industry are vulnerable to.

This is precisely what happened to Dr. Lloyd Wallin and his dental office in Burnsville, Minnesota in 2015. They had fallen victim to not one, but two cyber-attacks within a month. The doctor was left with a choice—pay $1,000 in exchange for decrypting the patient data base so it was accessible to employees. The cyber-attacker encrypted the patient database, which included:

• Patient records
• X-rays
• Schedules
• All patient data necessary to run the practice

No one could access this information, so what choice was there, aside from paying the fee? Dr. Wallin paid it and access was restored. Later that same month, it happened again, and this time he paid a second ransom of $600.

Once it's noted that you'll pay ransom, you become a bigger target for repeat attacks.

Dental offices are not the only ones vulnerable. In 2016, Dr. Rhee's medical office located in Tampa, Florida was hit with a common ransomware virus known as Locky. This malicious software infiltrated his systems in a stealth-like manner and hid in the background as it encrypted the data.

After the patient files were taken hostage, the cyber-attacker demanded money in return for decrypting files in his office. However, Dr. Rhee's outcome would be quite different.

Dr. Rhee had security backups that were consistently being performed, and he was able to restore files without paying thousands of dollars in ransom.

While there will always be cybercriminals trying to find an entry into a business's system, there is action that you can take to have a different outcome than paying ransom—again and again.

WHY THE HEALTH CARE INDUSTRY IS A BIG TARGET FOR CYBER CRIME

Ransomware and other types of malware/virus are not the only cybersecurity risk to healthcare organizations.

All types of data breaches are becoming more frequent in the healthcare industry. In 2015, there were over 112 million records involved in data breaches—just one year's worth of activity! It's estimated that approximately six billion dollars is lost annually due to data breaches. It's a big money business to be a cybercriminal.

Many cybersecurity experts believe that with the credit card data becoming less valuable due to enhanced chip and pin technology, healthcare data has become more valuable and will be stolen more frequently in the future. According to James Scott, co-founder and senior fellow at the Institute for Critical Infrastructure Technology (ICIT), "electronic health records are 100 times more valuable than stolen credit cards." He also noted that while numerous safeguards exist for financial information, fewer protections exist for health data, which is much more valuable. How valuable you ask?

Some experts have said that medical records go for anywhere between $500 and $900 each on the black market.

In 2017, the Washington University School of Medicine was a victim of a phishing attack. An employee had responded to an email that appeared legitimate, but was ultimately designed to infiltrate their systems by obtaining passwords of staff members email accounts. Those email accounts have access to protected health information (PHI) for 80,000+ patients. The data on here is a goldmine, as it contains:

- Names
- Birthdays
- Diagnoses
- Social Security numbers
- Insurance information
- Other sensitive data that a cybercriminal can use

Law enforcement had to be called in and a thorough investigation was conducted. This is required by the Department of Health and Human Services (HHS). Much of the regulation around how medical practices need to manage confidential information on their networks is covered through the Health Insurance Portability and Accountability Act, also known as HIPAA, whose compliance is run through HHS.

The investigation isn't only to find the source of the breach, but also to indicate whether the healthcare company (whether a medical services provider or third party vendor) had the proper technologies in place to protect the valuable data they are responsible for.

> *Are you wondering why anyone would want this information, and why it's of value? This information is valuable for the crime of identity theft, in particular. With a bit of information, someone can recreate you and use your name, history, and credit to score big in their crime.*

Far too many doctors and medical industry businesses know how damaging the consequences of a breach can be. Depending on its severity, they may be subject to fines and penalties that put them out of business. If the business can afford it, they may try to compensate by offering credit monitoring for a period of time. But either way, once there is a breach of HIPAA compliance or unsecured Protected Health Information (PHI), patients need to be notified in written form by mail or email.

If the practice has insufficient or out-of-date contact information for ten or more patients, the practice must post a notice on the home page of its website for ninety days or publish a notice in a newspaper or broadcast media in the area where patients reside. Further information can be found on the HHS.gov website. This is the part of the crime where your reputation can sustain extensive damage. Depending on the size of your healthcare company, it could be that final hit that eventually forces you out of business.

A FOCUS ON PREVENTION IS THE BEST ASSURANCE OF PROTECTION

The technology and training does exist to protect businesses who work in the medical industry from cybercriminals.

As you've learned, the ramifications of a breach to your medical or dental office are immense. Let's turn our attention to how we can prevent such attacks. These nine technology-best practices will help your business to reduce the risk of breach or attack, while also helping ensure your computer systems run more efficiently and smoothly:

1. **Perform consistent and regular backups.**
   Some forms of malware also target the backups, in which case your best defense is to have multiple backups, and in specific, use data backup to a cloud or offsite service such as Carbonite or Mozy, both of which are HIPAA complaint and adhere to strict security policies.

2. **Test restores to confirm they are successful.**
   Set up a schedule to test that backup systems are working. You never want to find out that your recovery plan from a breach isn't working—after the breach. Conduct a test restore at a minimum of once a month.

3. Restrict administrator-level access on workstations and servers.

Only those users who specifically need certain levels of information should have access to it. The principle of least privilege (POLP) mandates that employees are given the lowest level of user rights that allow them to do their job. Create separate user logons for each computer—one for the staff to use (non-admin level) and another one for the IT pro or practice manager's exclusive use. Through this privileged user login, your IT partner can install software and make operating system changes.

4. Conduct a risk assessment.

A risk assessment is necessary to evaluate and identify weaknesses within your network and infrastructure that are vulnerable to an attack or data breach. A reputable IT consulting firm or Managed Service Provider (MSP) will be able to help you with this assessment. On the final risk assessment report, you will see the best practices recommendations, and you should commit to implementing them as quickly as possible to protect the business and prevent an attack.

5. Educate users on the security policies of the medical or dental office.

Training is the critical piece to the puzzle. Practices should educate their employees on what a phishing email looks like and what a spoofed browser looks like. This will enable employees to be cautious when they receive a weird or unusual email and what actions to take. It's important to note that most cyber breaches are due to employee error so this type of information and education is necessary.

6. Apply security updates to all devices (e.g., desktops, laptops, servers, firewalls) on a regular basis, preferably on a monthly maintenance cycle.

This will allow you to address any vulnerabilities such as WannaCry or other ransomware or malware, before any exploits are discovered and to be protected against data loss. Your MSP or IT services company can help you with this, as they have tools to automate this process and make it much less cumbersome to implement.

7. **Use multi-factor authentication (also known as two-factor authentication).**
This provides an additional layer of protection and thwarts attacks, and is recommended for those who access sensitive data. Most applications require only one factor for authentication: a password. However, there are other ways to authenticate, such as a:
   • Fingerprint scan
   • Retina scan
   • Object such as hardware token
   • One-time code sent as text to your cell phone
The use of two or more authentication methods can take many forms, and some examples of companies providing this technology are RSA, Vasco Identikey, and Symantec VIP.

8. **Be alert if you are experiencing an attack in real time.**
If a malware or virus attack just happened, quickly disconnect the machine from the network to prevent it from infiltrating your network and propagating to other machines on your network.

9. **Limit physical access to technology.**
Some cybercriminals will walk right into your business through the use of social engineering (example: they pretend they are the "new IT guy"). Through having policies in place and restricting physical access to your servers or data center you're taking an extra security measure. Put a lock on the area, if possible.

10. **Properly store PHI.**
Storing PHI data on laptops, USB flash drives, mobile devices, or external hard drives is highly discouraged. Keep

these points in mind:

- If you must use a USB or thumb drive, make sure that it is encrypted. The hardware-encrypted flash drives are a good choice, preferably with FIPS 140-2 level 3 certification. You'll want to look for something that utilizes AES 256-bit encryption rather than CBC and other block cipher modes.
- Use USB devices that contain an on-board anti-virus to guard against viruses, malware, and spyware.

Any workstations containing PHI data should be encrypted using a program like Symantec Endpoint Encryption (also known as PGP) to ensure that any lost or stolen drives can't be accessed. This additional piece of software will protect the privacy and security of data containing protected health information (PHI). If you need to transfer any data with PHI between computers, it is important to use a SFTP client like WinSCP and use a SFTP server. These tools allow the data to be encrypted in transit. Without them, it is possible for the data to be intercepted on the network.

BE PROACTIVE

Taking a proactive stance instead of responding to a crisis is the best way to effectively manage your medical practice or healthcare organization.

There is a great deal to take into consideration when you are evaluating the technology decisions for your medical office or healthcare organization. It's an intensive, important process, and that means that having a fruitful conversation with an IT professional that is highly trained in HIPAA compliance and cyber-attack prevention is a smart choice.

This investment of your time and resources upfront is an important one to make. When your technology runs smoothly, it leaves you to do what you do best, taking care of your patients and the data they entrust you with.

About Maria

Maria Levin helps small and mid-sized businesses leverage technology to produce considerable gains in productivity and efficiency. With over 20 years of technology experience, she is passionate about technology and feels strongly that IT can be used to free employees from doing mundane and tedious tasks. Her philosophy is centered around a focus on continuous improvement and root-cause analysis to identify and resolve issues to prevent them from re-occurring in the future.

Maria earned an undergraduate degree in Computer Science from the University of New York at Albany, and a Master's degree in Business Administration (MBA) from Boston University. She has worked for various Fortune 500 companies, ranging from those in healthcare to finance industry, and has spent the last few years focused on consulting medical and dental offices in the CT area, specifically around cybersecurity and HIPAA-related challenges.

She is the Founder and President of Terabyte Tech Solutions, a Managed Service Provider (MSP) based in Old Greenwich, CT, offering technology implementation and support for desktops, servers, firewalls and networks, backups, training and security-related assessments.

You can find Maria at:
- Info@terabytetechsolutions.com

CHAPTER 10

IS MY DATA SAFE IN THE CLOUD?

BY MATT WEAVER

My business's slogan is "Freedom Through Technology" because I believe people should be able to work where they want, when they want. Even as a seasoned technology professional, I strongly believe there is always a time to unplug and put the technology away. I'm a big proponent of time spent outdoors without all the dings, buzzes, and never-ending email chains. I also believe, if the need arises, you should be able to grab your phone or preferred device from wherever you are and access systems and applications – which previously required you to be stuck in a seat in a stuffy office under florescent lights.

Four years ago, such a situation occurred while I was on my honeymoon. I was so love-struck with my beautiful bride, I'd forgotten to approve the invoices our accountant would need to send out while I was away. When I got the call from the office that the invoices due to be sent were missing my approval, I was able to simply borrow my wife's iPad to access our AgileCloudDesk. I clicked a few buttons to send approvals for billing and went back on my merry way to the pool deck of our cruise ship. I still prefer to do most of my work at my own desk in my office, but having access to the same exact desktop from anywhere I am has added a great amount of flexibility to my life, my business, and clients' businesses.

All my company's core business applications are now securely cloud-hosted. Should an emergency arise that requires my assistance, my team will contact me and I can carry out most of my duties on my cell phone. Our phone system is a cloud-hosted VOIP system which allows me to receive calls and transfer them to the appropriate person, no matter where I am located.

Cloud computing is not a new technology, but a combination of many old ones. What has really brought the term "Cloud" to the forefront in recent years is simply increased connectivity and marketing. Forget about the term "cloud" and consider that most computer systems these days are connected to the Internet and interact in various ways. Many people are on the cloud and using it without even knowing it, and they have been since before "cloud" was a buzz word. Things like Gmail, Hotmail, and other online services are cloud-based services. The cloud is not anything new from a technological perspective. Email servers have been around for decades, as have servers in datacenters. The operation of both of these is basically cloud computing. The difference is how we're accessing them, utilizing them, and the power they are able to deliver with little-to-no capital expense.

How is Data Safer in the Cloud than in my Office?

For some reason, people tend to feel safer when their data is physically near them, whether it is on their laptop or a server in their broom closet. Many people feel more secure with close physical proximity to their data than when putting their data in the cloud. In truth, it does depend on the cloud (more on that later), but the server in the broom closet is already connected to the Internet. It is most likely already accessible over the Internet. The difference between the server in a broom closet and the server in a datacenter (cloud) is that the server in the datacenter resides in a controlled environment, behind biometric security and various other protections, which are simply not feasible or cost effective in even the newest office buildings.

Some skeptics still may wonder, *"okay, the data center has impressive cyber security standards in place but what about a physical disaster, like fire?"* Datacenters have all kinds of fire-protections in place, but just in case a meteor hits a datacenter destroying it completely, the data should also live elsewhere. A proper cloud solution will house the data in multiple datacenters. Data should never live in only one physical location. The bottom line is that done properly, a cloud solution is undoubtedly MORE secure than an on-premise solution.

I work with a client who has roughly 150 employees, 50 of whom are desk jockeys with computers. This client has worked with several IT service providers in the past, but continued to suffer outages and lost data. This killed productivity and caused long weeks of catching up. When I first began speaking with this business, they were surprised my firm would work with them as if we were their own internal IT department, owning all problems. Even after being reassured the service would be impeccable, they were hesitant with the word "cloud," citing security concerns. To them, their data was more secure sitting on a physical server in the corner of the break room, where they could see it, touch it, and at least be aware of its presence humming away. I did insist we at least install a backup system with offsite replication (cloud backup.) The cloud backup could perform a function called "cloud virtualization." They agreed and it was their first step into the "cloud."

Two years later, the business was a very happy client, but an employee still had more access than they should and managed to download and install a virus called CryptoLocker. The virus not only encrypted the data on their local computer to hold it for ransom; it also encrypted the entire server since the employee's account had more network access than most. The business was panicked as their whole operation came to a grinding halt.

Thankfully, there was no real reason to worry because, with one phone call to my company, we had their whole operation up and running in the cloud from the offsite backup. Systems were connecting to the virtualized cloud backups, just as they had connected to the local server. After that, the client began to understand that just because a server is physically near them and on premise; it does not mean it is safe. Something on-premise, even with all of the proper firewalls, antivirus, and other safeguards, can rarely be more secure than data sitting in a properly secured data-center with controlled physical access, multiple data and power feeds, as well as the usual firewalls, and other safeguards.

Our client has seen the light and is now in the process of moving their entire digital infrastructure to a private cloud in a secure datacenter. This will give them MORE uptime and MORE security, as well as the flexibility of the service being billed like a utility, which can grow as the company grows.

What are the different formats of the Cloud?

There are three main cloud formats —
  (i) public
  (ii) private
  (iii) hybrid

Each one has pros and cons to consider when deciding which is best for your business.

Let's dive into the **public cloud**, which can be thought of like a utility. There is not much customization possible for each individual client, and the service provider's product either meets your needs or it does not. Decisions regarding which public cloud to use are often made on broad feature-sets and price, similar to choosing your TV provider at home. Public clouds tend to run across multiple servers in one or more datacenters, with any number of clients or users across servers. It is built to be scalable for the service provider to please the most people possible at a cost point the provider considers profitable, typically in a take-it-or-leave-it fashion.

Like the public cloud, **private clouds** are housed in datacenters and accessible over the Internet. The main difference is that a private cloud is designed for a specific client or user. Servers may be dedicated or virtual, but data remains local to the private cloud and is not in "pooled" storage across other users. When done properly, a private cloud offers greater flexibility for most business needs and arguably better security than a public cloud, as there is significantly more control over the configuration, storage, and accessibility.

While the cloud is ever-growing and constantly adding new security, features, and greater accessibility, there are still some information technology functions for which there are no benefit to putting in the cloud. In most businesses, there will most likely be at least some kind of on-premise component in addition to the physical local network such as switches, printers, monitors, and keyboards that do not make sense to put in the cloud. In some cases, a local print server or a local AutoCAD or Video Editing workstation may make sense. These are things that could be made to function in the cloud if enough resources and money are thrown at them, but the return on investment would likely be insignificant. Luckily, the technology used to make the "cloud" function is very versatile, and a good cloud integrator will be able to seamlessly integrate those on-premise and cloud services into a **"hybrid" cloud**.

It is important to note that while some services are available in the public cloud, the private cloud versions can offer far better service. For example, there are public file share services such as DropBox which are sometimes adequate, but there are also private file-share services that exist in private clouds which provide user-control over encryption keys and data storage. Private cloud services typically offer more features, such as securely mapping shared drives from on-site and cloud servers. They can join the worlds and add offline mobility as well, which certain businesses, such as our construction clients who work in the field, find helpful. The same goes for hosted desktop, which can be custom built in a "public cloud" on shared servers, but are often best to build out in datacenters where the fiber is owned and dedicated between them. This provides better connectivity and security.

TIPS FOR SECURING YOUR DATA IN THE CLOUD

1. **Choose a secure provider.** Ask the provider lots of questions to find out exactly how and when data is encrypted to ensure it is secure. All data must be encrypted in transit and preferably also at "rest." You do not want to be easy prey for a hacker. Make sure the provider tells you how and where data is stored and how it moves between your business and that location. Find out what controls are in place over who can access and process the data and what exactly the provider does with the data. Remember, not all providers are equal and there is no guarantee data will be handled securely just because you hire an IT provider.

2. **Back up in multiple locations.** Make sure your data is backed up in more than one location. Ideally, it should be backed up in at least two geographically-redundant data centers. Cloud technology, in its most basic form, is remote processing. Good cloud services are not housed in one building but sometimes across states, countries, and even continents to provide security by storing information across dispersed locations. If a tornado was coming through, you wouldn't want your data backed up in two data centers in the same town. Another good strategy is to always backup the cloud to the ground and ground to the cloud. When backing up data locally, the data must be encrypted, otherwise it is no longer secure. There's no point in having a secure cloud, if you're going to load personally identifiable information onto a USB stick for backup, which can easily be dropped

on the street corner for someone to find.

3. **User STRONG passwords and two-step verification.** Passwords MUST be strong, not your birthday, your address, or your kids' names. In fact, strong passwords are often no longer effective alone. No password is strong enough for a seasoned cybercriminal. Brute force can eventually crack almost any password. Two-step verification is vital. An example of simple two-step verification is having a user name, password, and then code texted to your phone which you must enter to complete the login process. An even better option is to use a Time-based One-time Password Algorithm (TOTP) service which can be a small piece of hardware, typically the size of a car key fob so it will easily fit on a key chain; or it can be an application on your phone such as Google Authenticator or Authy. This device will display a one-time user code that matches what the cloud system is expecting at the moment you login. Even if a hacker has your username and password, they'd be unable to login without knowing the code the device is displaying. It provides a strong second layer of protection. Cloud is secure but only as secure as the user makes it.

4. **Choose a cloud provider who offers a clear contract.** The contract between your business and the cloud provider should state the nature of your relationship, and most importantly, that the data belongs to your company, and your company alone, not the cloud provider. If the relationship is severed, the data should be returned to you to do with what you wish. Make sure the contract provides a clear exit strategy. If you aren't happy with the services or for some reason you need to cancel, what will be the process to return your data or transfer it to a new provider? Will you get your data in downloadable format? Do you get a copy of actual servers or just the data? Ideally, the cloud provider will allow you to access the actual virtual machines that make up your cloud. In a private cloud, the machines are customized for and dedicated to each client. If you're able to access the machines, not only will that give you access to the data, but

also the logins and usage records, hosted applications, and other configurations that may be custom to your business, simplifying your migration to another provider.

While the Cloud may sound like a new fad, it is not. Cloud is simply storing and processing information in remote data centers, accessed across the Internet. It is a firmly-rooted and well-used IT function with the addition of a flashy new name and a lot of media attention. The cloud is now being used across entire business systems to provide greater connectivity and security. Yet, many people are still fearful of the cloud because they think it is new and they cannot see or touch it; but you now know better. When done properly, the Cloud far exceeds onsite data storage and management, especially when it comes to security. If you haven't done so already, it is time to take action and learn about moving your business to a secure Cloud provider.

About Matt

Matt Weaver is founder and president of Agile Business Systems. He authored the book, *The Executive's Guide to Finding the Right Technology Consultant* – first published in 2010 (2nd edition published in 2016).

Founded in 2001, Agile Business Systems is a Pittsburgh-based technology firm focused on helping organizations grow through essential business technologies. After years of honing his skills in the enterprise world, Matt became aware of the gap in technology between large corporations and small- to medium-sized businesses. He founded Agile to bridge that gap, allowing organizations to enjoy the advantages that large corporations have, growing Agile Business Systems into the premier technology provider in the Greater Pittsburgh area.

With the advent of cloud technology, Matt is focused on cloud and security-first strategies which use virtualization technology to enable his clients to grow and spread their operations across multiple locations in ways that were previously quite cumbersome.

On days away from the office, Matt enjoys spending time with his wife and growing family (currently a 3-year-old boy, 1-year-old girl, and a third arriving shortly), or doing any outdoor activity from off-roading vehicles across the U.S. to running Tough Mudders.

You can connect with Matt at:
- MattW@AgileBusinessSystems.com
- www.linkedin.com/in/matthew-j-weaver
- www.AgileBusinessSystems.com | 412-308-5094

CHAPTER 11

TARGETED: WHY CYBERCRIMINALS LOVE YOUR BUSINESS

BY MICHAEL GLASSER
– Founder of Glasser Tech, LLC

After a fun and busy weekend, Jordan Rockstone, Senior Partner of Smythe, Rockstone, Johnstone, and Smithson, arrived at work. It was going to be a busy week and every minute was accounted for, but he was up to the challenge. Business meant money, and money paid the bills, after all.

He walked into the office at 6:30 AM, flipped the lights on, and went right to work. There was a contract for one of their largest clients, Stratosphere Properties, which needed attention first thing. Jordan logged into his computer, checked his emails, and then opened up the latest document in Microsoft Word. At least he tried to. It would not open.

Jordan grumbled and then began the tedious process of closing all the applications on his computer and preparing to reboot it. *This computer is glitching more and more*, he thought. There was always an issue, and always at the wrong time. Frustrated, Jordan began the process of closing all the applications and restarting the computer. It was less than a year old so there was no excuse for these things to be happening. He didn't care if it was software, hardware, or something else creating the issues. He just wanted it fixed, and for the IT company to get it right.

A half hour later...the reboot still hadn't fixed the problem.

By 7:00 AM, Jordan was boiling. He didn't care how early it was, he called the Office Manager, Sueann, to express his dismay about the "bleeping" computer people who were ripping them off and didn't know what they were doing.

When Jordan finally stopped for a breath, Sueann said she was almost at the office and she'd check on it first thing. He needed to calm down. Then she added, "Maybe you're just doing something wrong."

That didn't go well. "I'm just trying to open a document and do some work," Jordan retaliated. It didn't solve anything, but his ranting seemed necessary. He needed his computer fixed, period.

When Sueann arrived at the office she set her things down and started to log into her computer so she could retrieve Jordan's contract. She had no luck. Now it was Sueann's turn to start the reboot ritual, remembering the firm's IT motto: "When in doubt, reboot your PC."

Now there were two locked computers that wouldn't allow any documents to open. It was already 7:30 AM and everyone was beginning to arrive at work. Sueann's email, which was working, was lit up with messages from disgruntled employees expressing how they couldn't open up their documents.

Chaos had erupted!

Sueann made a call to All Things IT's help desk for support. She'd have to wait, though, because it wasn't 8:00 AM yet. In the background "new message" alerts kept blinking from the corner of her monitor. She messaged the IT company and rolled her eyes. *These guys were supposed to make things easier, but there was nothing easy about this.*

Finally, a connection was made. The problem could be solved!

Dan, one of the principal partners of All Things IT called Sueann and reassured her that he would look into the issue as quickly as he could and then get back to her.

In the back of Dan's mind, he had a hunch, but he didn't want to indicate anything until he knew for certain. He'd been down this road before…five times in the past few months actually. Those cases had all been ransomware. Would this one be too? He'd been proactive to try and help, convincing a handful of clients to move to cloud backups for part of their disaster recovery programs. But a handful had resisted, including this firm.

As he performed his investigation, Dan determined two things:
1) It was ransomware.
2) He knew which PC had started the infection.

From his remote location, Dan attempted to power off the suspect's PC to isolate the problem, but he was unable to do so. Now he had to make the call—the one that was never pleasant.

"Sueann, Dan here. You've been 'hit' with ransomware and I'll need to restore the systems."

"Where did it come from?" Sueann asked, glancing toward Jordan in his office.

"Blaine Smithson's computer was the point of entry; maybe an email or infected website."

Then Dan gave Sueann instructions to immediately turn off and disconnect Blaine's PC manually, right down to unplugging it. He reassured her that it was good that they at least had a backup plan, even if it was without the cloud, and that he felt they could get them back up and running fairly quickly.

"But we have 50 staff members who'll all be here soon. Can you move more quickly?" Sueann asked. Her mind flashed to the horror of mobs of workers approaching her like angry villagers with pitch forks.

"I'll do the best I can," Dan said, and he meant it, but there was a lot to do.

Sueann ended the call and made the walk to Jordan's office. He was on the phone and staring at his PC. He hung up when he saw her, and she informed him of what was going on and when he asked what happened, she repeated what Dan had told her.

"Don't we pay money every month to All Things IT to take care of our security?" Jordan asked, noticeably surprised.

What could Sueann say? She just relayed the information about Dan's confidence in quickly restoring the system and that they were fortunate they had some disaster recovery in place.

Jordan didn't feel better. What about the tens of thousands of dollars per hour they might be losing? And how about all those documents? The deadlines...his thoughts went on and on, bombarding him to the point of the stress being written all over his face and evident in his voice.

Someone came to Sueann and said Dan from All Things IT was on the phone. She rushed over and Dan said, "Things are complicated. The hackers have taken over the onsite backup system with ransomware. I need to come up with Plan B."

When an IT disaster takes place, not having a comprehensive plan in place equals stress and uncertainty for a business.

Breaking the news to Jordan was not fun for Sueann, or anyone in earshot. Jordan bellowed loudly, frustrated about his expectations about IT's role with the situation he was in.

"I'm going to fix this myself," Jordan said. He googled "ransomware recovery" and saw pages of websites and ads come up that specialized in the service. One of the data recovery websites, TRUDATA, had a fair number of positive Google reviews and mentioned their speedy service, professionalism, and good results. Jordan picked up the phone and dialed 1-800-TRU-DATA. Someone answered immediately.

Five minutes later he'd paid a deposit of $10,000.00 on the company's AMEX and was eager for them to arrive and recover his system. William from TRUDATA would be there by 10:30 AM.

Afterward, he called out to Sueann, who came rushing in, and told her to call Dan and tell him to be at the office at 10:30 AM—or else.

Once Sueann was gone from the office, Jordan crumbled. He was embarrassed about such a thing happening at his firm. What if word got out? What would their clients think? And prospective clients? All the questions gave him a migraine, and he squeezed his eyes shut, trying to calm his raging fears.

He barely felt better by the time Dan and William arrived.

The process of recovery began and everyone, while behind, was finally relieved.

Dan explained the customer situation to William, with Jordan listening, his jaw tense. William suggested that he get right to work and they sign him into the servers and workstations so he could make notes and analyze the infected systems.

"We have Cyber Liability Insurance. Why can't we just pay the ransom from my insurance policy and get back to work?" It seemed logical. That was what the insurance was for, right?

William asked Jordan for a copy and he provided it, and he began to read through it, pointing out a specific clause.

"This policy specifically excludes lost productivity and ransom payments. It only covers the costs of remediation to restore the environment."

Breathing in and trying to think rationally, Jordan thought about the massive amounts of revenue he was losing by having the ransomware demand go unmet. He literally was being held hostage and saw no means of negotiation. He had to pay.

The ransom demanded by the hackers was 100 bitcoins, over $100,000 at the current exchange rates.

Jordan asked one more time. "Dan, why can't I recover my backups?"

"It seems that the hackers have been in the systems a while and they've taken control of the local backups. They are all compromised and can't be restored."

"I can't believe with all this money I am paying for IT support that I can't get my files back!" Jordan protested. "I can't be down for days, unable to operate my business. I am going to pay the ransom and sort it out after I'm up and running again."

"I would be very careful about that, Mr. Rockstone," William cautioned. "Paying the ransom doesn't guarantee you'll actually get your files back. You could be throwing your money away.

I recommend waiting until we understand more about what happened."

Dan agreed.

As for Jordan Rockstone, his face turned flush so quickly that you would have thought the temperature in the room had rapidly climbed to 120°.

Whether it was good luck or dumb criminals, good news was received. The ransomware could be decrypted.

William had been scouring the systems when he realized that they could decrypt the ransomware and restore all the information. He was excited, but not as excited as Jordan. "Do it! Get me back to work!" Jordan felt invincible at that moment, like he'd taken down the bad guys. It was awesome.

By 3:00 PM, all of the systems had been decrypted and restored to good working order. Jordan called Dan and William into his office. "Dan, I want you to put a new solution in place right now to protect my onsite backups from damage, and I want to be on the cloud thing you mentioned."

William replied. "Mr. Rockstone, we're not finished with the investigation. We cannot be sure the bad guys have been evicted from your system yet. We really should take a backup of your system now and hold that offline...just in case."

"Just do whatever it takes," Jordan said.

William and Dan nodded and got back to work, leaving one Jordan Rockstone in his office, feeling pleased. He'd been threatened to pay $100,000 to a criminal and had just solved his problem for a fraction of that price.

It was already the end of the day and he went home, celebrated his ability to command the situation, and woke up bright and early to get to work. Now he was in "catch-up mode".

A new day with a new opportunity had arrived.

When Jordan Rockstone arrived at work the next day he had a spring in his step as he turned on his computer. He was deflated when he read the message across his screen: *ransom not paid on time. Your files have been removed.*

Just like Ground Hog's Day, everything began to repeat itself. Sueann called Dan and William and they were there within an hour. But this time they had an edge. Although the systems had been wiped out, it could be recovered from the offline backup.

Jordan was embarrassed again, but he'd learned a lesson. After everything was restored again, he asked what could be done to stop what had happened to the firm from happening again. He was willing to invest in whatever it took to find a permanent solution.

To fully understand the solutions to these types of security issues, it required a full day meeting, but it was one that Jordan knew would be worth his time. He could not afford to be negligent with his firm's data and resources. The solution was a five-point plan that included:

1. A Written Information Security Policy (WISP), which is a referral source for all employees, helping them to understand how to protect critical office resources.
2. A thorough review of the cyber insurance policy to ensure the firm understood all the details of their policy, for all areas—especially paying ransom.
3. Training classes for staff to help them understand how to avoid social engineering and phishing attacks, as well as all the ways that criminals can turn a seemingly harmless activity into an open door for a cyber breach.
4. Implementing additional security measures such as a firewall

security suite, improved intrusion detection, and enhanced security software.

5. An updated Disaster Recovery Plan (DRP) that incorporated their new technologies and security measures. This plan addressed critical information for the firm in regards to acceptable downtime, data loss, frequency of backups, and a specific plan for returning the business to normal operations, should an event occur.

Additionally, the coordinated efforts between Dan and William to establish best practices for the firm were a guide to prevention that the firm needed. Jordan's willingness to invest in technology that offered the required protection for the firm and work environment made the difference. Without training and technology, it is very hard to safeguard data on computers and protect it from breaches and ransomware requests.

Other things the firm was cautioned to be mindful about included:

- Quarterly reviews of all security policies
- Protecting all Personally Identifiable Information (PPI) so it cannot be accessed by unauthorized individuals
- Systems in place for encrypting data that was at rest or in transmission
- Subscribing to a cyber monitoring service that would allow for rapid detection of breaches or attempted breaches, as well as immediate remediation of threats
- System checkups that ensured the backup data was operating efficiently and to expectations

The story in this chapter is true. In fact, it happened on the day I began writing this chapter. A single unqualified IT person from another company hadn't covered all the bases necessary, leaving critical gaps in the system that lead to two ransomware attacks in less than six months. We were pleased to be able to solve their problems when they finally contacted us, and offer them better processes to prevent any future attacks.

Proactive businesses take action so they don't become a statistic. At Glasser Tech's website (http://glassertech.com/security), we offer a checklist of actionable security measures.

Assessing your vulnerability and risk today is the first step in making sure you aren't facing a breach that is hard, if not impossible, to recover from "someday". There is never a convenient day or time for a breach.

About Michael

Michael Glasser is the owner and founder of Glasser Tech, LLC, a Computer Consulting Firm, operating since 2008. Michael grew up with the computer revolution. In 1987, he graduated from Hofstra University with a degree in Finance, but it's his love for the computer industry that keeps him 'ahead of the curve' by constantly looking for industry trends to bring value to his clients.

You can visit Glasser Tech's website (http://glassertech.com/security) for a checklist of actionable security measures.

Because of Michael's numerous certifications with Legal Industry-specific applications, Glasser Tech offers a unique consultative approach that enables law firms to maximize the integration of hardware and software to custom-tailor ideal solutions to meet specific customer needs. Michael is well known within the legal industry as a solutions provider and supports hundreds of law firms and thousands of systems with industry-specific technology solutions. Michael has put together a team whose many years of combined experience provides the utmost customer service.

Michael maintains the same level of passion, excitement and enthusiasm as he did when he started thirty years ago, as a teenager. Other interests he enjoys include fitness, yoga and outdoor activities.

CHAPTER 12

SOCIAL ENGINEERING ATTACKS

BY MARK ELLIOTT

In March 2011, two small groups of employees at RSA Security received an email with the subject line "2011 Recruitment Plan." Although the message automatically ended up in junk mail folders, one employee thought it was worth his or her attention, pulled it out of that folder and opened the attached Excel spreadsheet, innocuously named "2011 Recruitment plan.xls." With that one simple click, the employee unknowingly unleashed malware that installed a backdoor into their computer by exploiting a vulnerability (since fixed) in Adobe Flash. The hackers were now in charge of the machine. They first stole several of the employee's passwords and used those to access other employees who had high access to sensitive information. Eventually, the hackers stole data associated with one of the RSA's security products, used at that time by 40 million businesses to keep their operations safe.

Think about that for a minute. One of the world's most respected computer security companies was successfully targeted by a "social engineering" attack. If it can happen to someone whose job is literally to protect data, it's doesn't take a big leap in logic to assume it can happen to anyone – and it has. Target, the FBI, eBay, and the Associated Press are just some of the high-profile institutions and entities that cyber-criminals have targeted with these kinds of breaches.

Research shows that social engineering has emerged as the No.1 data security threat and the preferred tool for hackers.

In one case alone, hackers conducted a social engineering attack which robbed 100 different banks, in nearly 30 countries, of one billion dollars over a two-year period.

WHAT IS "SOCIAL ENGINEERING"?

In the simplest terms, social engineering is a process in which hackers trick their targets into handing over sensitive data – passwords, logins, system configuration details, etc. Basically, it is a high-tech confidence game. Cyber-criminals try to exploit our natural tendencies (or weaknesses) through human interaction. They'll do whatever it takes – manipulation, influence, pressure, persuasion, greed – to get victims to make security errors that allow them to crack into computers, servers, and networks, or introduce malicious software or ransomware that can cripple operations and cost millions.

Thus, the name: Hackers depend on social contacts to engineer human behavior.

Social engineering takes many forms. Two of the more common are phishing and spear phishing. In a phishing attack, the hacker attempts to steal data by posing as a legitimate person, entity, or business. The target gets a seemingly innocent communication – generally an email or text message – with an attachment or link that looks legitimate. Clicking the link, the victim is directed to a website that has been created for the purpose of tricking them into surrendering sensitive information such as passwords or Social Security numbers. Clicking the attachment, as the RSA case illustrates, installs a malicious program. According to some estimates, 85 percent of organizations have reported being victims of phishing attacks. The 2014 Home Depot breach – in which hackers stole information from 56 million credit and debit cards – is believed to have been a phishing attack. Cyber-criminals accessed a vendor's log-on credentials to break into the company's network and install malware that harvested customer payment card data and emails.

Spear-phishing is a form of phishing. It occurs when the victim receives an email from someone he or she thinks they know. Trust is key. The cyber-criminal will call you by name, reference someone or something you may know, or otherwise demonstrate their "trustworthiness." Having established a connection, they'll encourage you to click on an attachment or link. When you do, malware will infect the computer and they will have gained backdoor access to your data.

A more sophisticated, and more targeted, variation of these is what's called "whaling." In these attempted breaches, the hacker finds a way into the network and then sends employees an email that looks like it came from a high-ranking company official, often the chief executive officer. The FBI, in an April 2016 warning, put it like this:

> The schemers go to great lengths to spoof company email or use social engineering to assume the identity of the CEO, a company attorney or trusted vendor. They research employees who manage money and use language specific to the company they are targeting, then they request a wire fraud transfer using dollar amounts that lend legitimacy... There are various versions of the scams. Victims range from large corporations to tech companies to small businesses to nonprofit organizations. Many times, the fraud targets businesses that work with foreign suppliers or regularly perform wire transfer payments.

Unfortunately, social engineering and spear phishing aren't the only weapons in the hacker's arsenal. Here are three other common ways they will try to breach your data:

Baiting: Similar to phishing, this occurs when the attacker promises victims something of perceived value – a free movie download, for example, or a free eBook – in exchange for critical information like passwords and login credentials. A variation of this is the *quid pro quo* attack, in which the attacker requests information in exchange for a service or benefit. We often see hackers posing as technology professionals, contacting employees with offers of free IT consulting services…if they agree to give up certain information.

Pretexting: By and large, all hackers lie in some regard – that's how they get what they want. But pretexting can be a bit more elaborate. Hackers will sometimes create realistic (but fictional) situations or fabricate entire identities designed to build trust; someone seemingly from your bank, for example, saying your credit card has been corrupted and asking for personal information to restore it. The unwitting target, hoping to solve the problem, provides the information without question – and the hacker goes to work.

Waterholing: This also relies on trust – but trust of a different kind. Whereas someone with an awareness of security might not open a suspect email or click a questionable link, they may not be quite so alert when it comes to websites they often visit (i.e., a favorite online watering hole). Hackers going after a clearly-defined group of people – let's say lawyers – go to popular legal sites, find vulnerabilities, and modify its code or infect it with malware. That malware then compromises whatever device or computer was used to access it, opening the door for cyber-criminals.

AVOIDING – OR OVERCOMING – A SOCIAL ENGINEERING HACK ATTACK

I always say most organizations or businesses exist in one of two states when it comes to protecting sensitive data: pre-crisis and crisis. The enterprise that is prepared for a breach stands a much better chance of avoiding – or at minimum, mitigating the effect of – a cyber-assault. I can say with absolute certainty that any business, organization, or individual that thinks they are immune to attacks because they have a firewall in place or installed anti-virus software, is whistling in the IT security graveyard.

So what can you do? It's a combination of training and technology.

As I noted earlier, it is important to remember the emphasis in social engineering is on "social" – human interaction. Hackers rely on basic human emotions, tendencies, or desires, to con people into going to suspect websites, downloading malware, opening poisonous attachments, or turning over sensitive information. Knowing this, it just makes sense to ensure that anyone with access to sensitive data has the skills, awareness, and education necessary to serve as a first line of defense.

Research shows nearly a quarter of all companies hit by a data breach said employee error was to blame. Despite that, a survey of corporate counsels found that less than half – 45 percent – of companies reported they conduct mandatory training designed to help employees prevent hack attacks. Interestingly, research shows that overconfidence in identifying phishing emails – the belief of victims that they are smarter than the hackers – is the No. 1 reason they fall prey to the cyber-criminal. If all that's not reason enough to enhance data security training, consider these statistics: More than 400,000 phishing sites were observed, on average, in each month during 2016, and their average lifespan is less than 15 hours. In other words, more sites are going up, and they're coming down faster than ever, making it difficult to detect, block, or kill them.

For the most part, employee training is a function of employee awareness. Yes, there are same basics, such as creating strong passwords to impede hackers and changing those passwords regularly. (Hints: Don't use predictable personal information such as a pet's name or a spouse's birthday as a login; phrases composed of 12 or so random words are a good defense against password cracking.) But the best strategy is to make sure potential victims understand how hackers hack and that they know what to do if they suspect an attempted breach. Here are some ways employees can improve, rather than impede, security:

- **Knowledge is power over hackers.** Educate employees on how to identify links, attachments, emails, web addresses, and online ads that might be suspect. If they do not know the sender, they should not even open or respond to the email – especially one caught in a spam filter – and they should never download documents or attachments from unknown senders.

- **Beware of what's in a name.** A study released in early 2017 found 91 percent of phishing threats analyzed came from "display name spoofs," in which the hacker disguises himself or herself as someone familiar to the victim. If there's any doubt about the name in the "from" line of an email, kill it.

- **Don't believe what you think you see.** Social engineering attacks often rely on our assumption that what we think we see is what we actually see. So hackers might transpose two letters, for example, in the "from" line, the body of an email, or the signature; the eye thinks it sees the correct spelling and believes the communication is legitimate. Similarly, if you see an email with obvious misspellings, bad grammar, or poor or low-resolution logos – none of which any respected brand would condone – you're likely encountering a bad actor.

- **Watch out for the tangled web addresses hackers weave.** Often, hackers will make an ever-so-slight change in a web URL in the hope you won't notice and will click through it.

As I have said repeatedly, that will start you down the path toward data theft, computer hijackings, malicious programs, and a range of other negative outcomes.

- **Don't let them have you at "hello."** If you receive an email that starts with words or phrases such as "Friend," "Hello," Devoted Banking Client," "Fellow IT Professional," etc., it is a potential indicator that some hacker is on a phishing expedition.
- **Avoid embracing the embed.** Never click on a link embedded in a suspect email. If you think it might be valid, enter the URL manually into the browser window.
- **Keep private information private.** While I realize this is a glaring statement of the obvious, it bears repeating. Don't surrender private personal information to anyone. Ever.
- **Patch things up.** It seems obvious, but is important to remember as the most obvious is often overlooked. Make sure employees are current on software patches that fix bugs which can be exploited. To take that a step further, develop an approved list of apps and software that employees can download.

Hackers are becoming more sophisticated, so even the best-trained employees can fall victim to their cons. That is when technology becomes a significant tool. It can not only prevent potential targets from becoming victims, but can also help to derail a breach before it has a chance to do any damage. Let me state clearly, this is not an either/or proposition. Securing your data requires effective technology as well as educated employees.

The need for speed

I believe one of the best, strongest technology weapons at the disposal of any enterprise is software that detects and deletes malware in real time. There are any number of off-the-shelf solutions that can do the detecting and deleting. The problem is that the process takes hours or even days; by that point, the damage is done. Since as many as 323,000 new malware files are identified every day, it stands to reason that the quicker you can find them and kill them, the better. This means applying software that finds and identifies viruses, bugs, and worms in a matter of minutes and then deletes them upon detection.

High catch rates
Consistent with the above, you want a program with a high catch rate. Unfortunately, most anti-virus (AV) products aren't up to the job. Too many products are to too slow in catching too few bugs. What you need is a product that has been proven to detect, as nearly as possible, 100 percent of attempted invasions and malware delivered through email; 100 percent of social exploits (software, data, or commands that exploit a vulnerability in a computer in order to, among other things, take it over); and 99 percent of attempted breaches. Anything less puts your enterprise at risk.

More layers are better
As referenced earlier, bad actors often go after emails as a back door into computers, servers, or networks. Multifactor authentications can be an effective way to protect data from this threat, by protecting a target's credentials. The concept is simple. Rather than employing a single tool (i.e., a password), users are validated through two or more layers of security. So in addition to passwords, the procedures might include PINs, one-time pass codes which expire after a few minutes, security questions, or biometric identifiers such as thumbprints or retina scans. Still, it's not perfect. RSA, the company whose hack was discussed at the beginning of this chapter, had a two-factor authentication system in place, and that didn't stop hackers. The lesson? More layers are better.

Social engineering is not going away anytime soon. Yes, we can train employees to identify threats. Yes, we can install software to detect malware. And yes, we can delete bugs and viruses. But hackers are like a disease that becomes resistant to a vaccine. As we keep finding solutions, hackers keep trying to find ways to get around them. This is not to suggest the fight is futile. It does, however, argue we must be aware, vigilant, relentless, and proactive in taking the fight to dirty players. Hackers believe that as long as there is a human factor, they'll win. But we can change the equation to our advantage. We can, and we should.

About Mark

As CEO and co-founder of 3i International, Mark Elliott has more than two decades of experience helping companies apply technology to improve their performance, processes, and profitability. He is a well-respected and widely known IT professional who has developed a comprehensive understanding of the office IT environment and how to maximize its potential.

As the driving force behind a number of high-growth companies, Mark has blended his IT and business experience to help clients develop effective – and cost-effective – strategies that support operational and bottom-line objectives. He has a broad-based understanding of how enterprises work from the inside, giving him proficiencies that go beyond IT alone to encompass relevant skills such as strategic planning, cash flow, and sales and marketing. As concerns over cyber-security have emerged, he has also become a recognized leader in data security and helping clients detect and defeat hacker attacks.

CHAPTER 13

MANAGING YOUR COMPANY DATA IN THE AGE OF MOBILE DEVICES

BY MICHAEL COOPERSMITH
– Integrated Technology Systems

As an owner or key manager within a business, you value the accessibility that mobile devices bring to employees and the workplace. However, this accessibility brings information security vulnerability, and spotlights how important it is to strengthen company controls over employees working on these devices.

Consider the following scenario, experienced by one of our clients:

- A disgruntled employee starts sending company-wide emails disparaging the owners, which leads to a hasty dismissal. However, when the owners look to wipe all business email and data from his phone, their lawyer stops them. Because there is no mobile strategy in place, his personal data would be wiped as well, and they would face being sued.

Or, a few more examples:

- Your employee's phone is lost, and has no password protection in place – email and other information is available to anyone who picks it up.
- Your employee's teenager borrows the tablet the parent uses for work apps, visiting gaming sites that download malware onto the device. Most of the time this only interferes with the device, but it can also damage the data itself, and then move onto the network.

Mobile Device Management (MDM) and **Enterprise Mobility Management** (EMM) are terms business owners are seeing more frequently in business articles. With the explosion of mobile devices – both smartphones and tablets – and the desire to give companies access to their employees, and their employees anywhere/everywhere access to their work, this is one more area small and medium-sized businesses (the SMB market) need to proactively address. Otherwise, you lose control over access to your infrastructure and your data, and trying to "close the barn door" and contain damage that is already done can put your own client base or even your entire business at risk. Remember, your data is your business – your customer lists, contracts, key processes – these are all your intellectual property, and need to be protected.

You may not have heard as much about MDM and EMM as you have about firewalls, antivirus, passwords, phishing attacks, and malware – all bigger topics when it comes to the news media. It is all too common to see headlines like the 2013 Target security breach that resulted in 40 million cards exposed and 70 million customers' data stolen, or Cryptolocker stories, where thieves from remote corners of the world manage to reach into a company's data and extort payments to unlock it. However, that powerful minicomputer almost everyone carries – your phone, which has more processing power in the palm of your hand than the computer that filled an entire room a few decades ago –

represents a way in to your entire infrastructure.

Informing and educating businesses on how to ensure they are participating in the best mobile device practices for their business is no longer an option. As of this moment, your business is in one of these two scenarios: 1) you are required to have specific safeguards in place for mobile technology; or 2) new laws or compliance guidelines are on the horizon in the near future. In a busy work environment that involves your daily tasks, budgeting, training, and paying attention to your valuable business data, you really don't have time to waste.

Whether employees are working on their own or on corporate-owned devices, it is almost impossible to track employee mobile activities in real time. Here are three reasons for SMBs to develop a mobile device usage strategy:

1 - While cybercrime against big companies make the headlines, smaller companies represent easier, softer targets to cybercriminals – and the financial impact to smaller companies is just as devastating.

2 - Cybercriminals are working 24 hours a day to exploit any access possible, so even if malware directed at mobile devices is not the primary driver today for an EMM policy, it could well be in the near future. With use of a mobile device – which resides outside your network, downloading infected apps or software patches, or visiting compromised websites or malware popups – these online activities can infect your devices with malware and viruses that can compromise sensitive corporate information.

3 - The negative financial impact to your company from a rogue employee with open mobile access to company data that is virtually un-auditable (or unregulated when your company is likely to become more accountable to more compliance) can be just as dangerous to your bottom line.

Who Owns the Device? COPE versus BYOD

As a business decision maker, you have two ownership models to consider for your mobile technology in the workplace:

- Corporate-owned, Personally-enabled (COPE): a company supplies mobile devices to their employees for business use (but can allow personal use).
- Bring Your Own Device (BYOD): individuals that supply their own mobile devices that they use for business functions, as well as personal use.

Which one is more beneficial for your business? It is estimated that more than 60% of businesses prefer BYOD, and that's a trend that keeps rising. What are the reasons for this? With COPE, you may be able to control more of what you allow employees to do with the device; however, with BYOD, not only are you saving on the purchase costs of mobile devices, but for employees, it is an issue of workplace autonomy. Employees have reported a greater sense of control over their work when using their own familiar devices; they often prefer to carry only one phone or tablet versus multiple devices, so work updates and team communication are more seamless and flexible.

So what is the difference between MDM and EMM?

MDM enables you to control and track which employees and what mobile devices can have access to applications your business uses, whether it is email, calendaring, or other lines of business software. For example, if you allow your employees today to access their email via their smartphones, do you have any idea how many devices they have installed it on? MDM gives you a way to approve or deny access from any device, and inventory which devices are still connected.

EMM controls the flow of the data moving within those

applications – by limiting access, separating company data from personal employee data, and allowing you to safely wipe that data if necessary. MDM fits into a broad, comprehensive EMM policy, which in turn should be part of a total network security/business continuity plan. Developing an EMM strategy addresses the company's security concerns and also provides the ability for employees to have access to the tools they need to be productive and efficient on smartphones and tablets – from anywhere. While safeguarding the employer's company and intellectual property, it respects the privacy of the users, which is mandated by law. It is illegal for you to be able to view their private information from your business platform. This includes social media accounts, banking information, private email, etc. However, your business's data is one of your greatest assets and you do have to safeguard it at all costs. This is required through compliance and by the law.

Do you know where you stand right now?

If you're unsure, consider these points:

- *What is your policy if a device were to be lost?* Someone who picks up the device should not be able to easily access the apps and portals that are business-related.
- *How do you handle employees who are fired or leave your firm?* You need to make sure that employees are not leaving with access to client data or your company's intellectual property.
- *What security features do you have in place to prevent hacking into the devices?* Many people are not mindful that their mobile devices are computers, and criminals who want the information those devices hold can hack into them.

MINIMIZING RISKS IN AN AGE OF INCREASING REGULATION

Because of their relationships with clients in regulated industries, there is a growing obligation for certain types of businesses, particularly legal and financial services, to themselves meet those compliance standards. This leads to policies in place for security of mobile devices. If these policies and practices are not in place, you may not be permitted to conduct business with certain enterprises. For the business that is not already prepared, this could mean:

A loss of potential clients: Our law firm clients who focus on the highly-regulated financial services sector are now consistently receiving compliance audit requests from their clients, and have been forced to adopt MDM policies and safeguards. Otherwise, their client relationships are at risk. Can your business afford that?

Risk of compliance violations: By not following the extensive compliance regulations that are important to your industry, you risk fines and potentially having to close your doors to business. The Health Insurance Portability and Accountability Act (HIPAA) and the Sarbanes-Oxley Act of 2002 (SOX) have intensive measures in regard to compliance and protection of any and all data—even that on mobile devices. Or if you're in the Payment Card Industry (PCI), you have to go through extensive measures to make sure you are processing payments in a manner that makes it tough, if not impossible, for consumers' data to get stolen. These are all imperative to a business's ability to thrive and they apply to: 1) mobile devices; 2) on-site devices; and 3) any third-party vendors you may use that have access to data.

You've worked hard to build your business and reputation. To lose it by not taking a proactive approach to MDM can be a critical mistake. If you do not have an internal CTO, a strong IT firm with mobile strategy expertise will help you with policy, training, the proper technologies, and monitoring of these devices.

SIX WAYS TO SAFELY USE MOBILE TECHNOLOGY

There are highly effective ways to integrate ease-of-use of a device with state-of-the-art security features. While one device for everything almost always wins the popular vote with employees, we have an obligation to have controls in place that ensure employee privacy and your right to protect company access and data.

1. **Containerize data**

   In order to ensure that personal and business data do not mix, you need to containerize the data. By doing this, you put "capsules" over business data used on the phone. In that capsule may be the word processing program, email, the cloud, applications for the business, etc. This way you isolate the business data, and if a device is stolen or an employee leaves the organization, you can immediately wipe only the company data.

2. **Proper set-up of devices**

   When you enroll a device in MDM, you can set the parameters so the phone has to have certain safety features in place to ensure protection of your business, while also meeting compliance guidelines. Additionally, with the proper set-up you can easily push out standard configurations, and also define which applications are deployed on the business side.

   - *Wi-Fi*: you can restrict a user in a way that they cannot use certain Wi-Fi networks (such as public ones) while they are using business tools—the ones that are containerized.
   - *Virtual Privacy Network (VPN)*: if an employee is connecting back to a company's network, you can limit which VPNs can be used from a device.
   - *Password restrictions*: mobile devices do not allow for two-factor authentication so you have to choose another route for safety. The most recommended is having a minimum of a six-digit code to access the phone, and

the apps within it that are business related. This code should be changed at least every ninety days for extra security.

3. Individual management

Most technology users today are fairly adept with navigating mobile technology, many having grown up with it. This means that something that may seem simple, such as letting your family member use your phone for something when you're out, shouldn't be done. Even going into business applications and leaving them open while you step away from your device for a moment should be discouraged. "Jailbreak" is also an issue, particularly on a BYOD device – tech-savvy employees can find ways to install restricted applications. These applications can increase the risk of data breach. Obviously, this is hard to control from any technology standpoint, as it involves human behavior and habits. To address these issues you must:

- Have your CTO or IT partner hold employee training on what's expected by the business and compliance demands for their mobile devices.
- Have signed documentation that the employee understands the expectations of them and the consequences if they violate the policy on file in their employment records.

4. Encryption

There are no excuses for not having every bit of information that is exchanged via a mobile device encrypted. This is what makes it unreadable to an unauthorized individual trying to access it.

5. Reports, policies, and best practices

Depending on the size of your business, you could find that you have a high number of devices to manage. Integrated Technology Systems has helped businesses of all sizes through guiding and assisting with:

- Device registration systems
- Inventories of all devices that have mobile access to business resources
- Reports on device usage to detect odd or suspicious behaviors and patterns
- Security reports to show failed log-in attempts, potential breaches, and potential "teachable moments"—those moments where it is time to update employee training on the devices at hand
- Ensuring that patches and updates on all systems and software on the phone are performed efficiently and regularly

6. **Be prepared for operations that need to be controlled by ownership and management**
   While a great IT resource is an integral part of setting up your security defenses for mobile technology, the company and its management must take responsibility for ensuring they can document and verify that everything is being done that is required from their end. This includes documentation of all efforts and information regarding the mobile technology. It also involves having written policies in place and documentation that shows employees know exactly where to find it.

PEACE OF MIND COMES FROM STRONG PARTNERSHIPS

MDM and EMM do not have to be complicated from a technical standpoint. You can take advantage of systems that have proven effective and offer relative ease in deployment of devices. This includes toolsets from large players in the industry; Microsoft has MDM pieces available in Office 365 and Intune, an EMM platform. Blackberry has pivoted from the smartphone business and reinvented itself as an EMM player by acquiring Good, which is a secure, containerized offering. IBM and VMWare are in the market as well, along with a number of smaller companies.

While you do need a CTO or a knowledgeable technology advisor to implement these solutions, they are all moving rapidly into the SMB market. These are important conversations that we have at Integrated Technology Systems regularly. When you have plans to do great business, you have to have a reliable technology plan in place. Don't worry if that's not your strength; find a reliable and experienced technology partner.

About Michael

Michael Coopersmith was the kid who put all of his family's stereo components together. He couldn't wait to get his hands on the neighborhood's first Commodore 64, and his first afterschool job included programming Lotus spreadsheets. He started his career as an accountant and then merged his experience with business and technology to assist companies in expanding the potential of IT.

Now, as CEO of ITS NYC, he leads his team of project managers and technicians, experts in providing reliable technology services to the small and mid-sized business community. They function as the outsourced IT department for law firms, accounting and financial firms, real estate companies and a broad range of other industries. Their proactive monitoring technologies, remote remediation, onsite support, team approach and flat rate service plans maximize their clients' network uptime while delivering predictable technology cost.

ITS NYC provides a range of hosting and cloud solutions to improve performance. Clients have access to leading business technology without considerable software and hardware expenses. ITS NYC's remote and local backup solutions protect company data, minimize business risk, and enable quick recovery of lost or damaged data. They have an impressive track record for business continuity and disaster recovery; just one day after Superstorm Sandy, half of their clients were up, and all were restored within a week.

ITS NYC's experience with HIPAA compliance and other regulatory oversight makes them adept at helping clients maintain or exceed legal requirements related to data security. They also have tools that provide companies with enhanced control and oversight of data, while providing access for their users for data sharing and remote work capabilities.

ITS NYC's clients view technology as an investment in productivity and efficiency. ITS brings the most effective IT tools available, customized to meet the specific needs of each client, and thus allows each to focus on running their core business.

When not working with his team and his clients, Michael travels to explore the outdoors with his family, and runs regularly with his sons. He and his oldest son have completed six half marathons, and are training for their first full marathon later this year. They often run in support of Achilles International, in appreciation for all Achilles has done to support disabled athletes worldwide.

CHAPTER 14

REAL-LIFE HACKING SCENARIOS AND HOW THEY COULD HAVE BEEN PREVENTED

BY LISA NIEKAMP-URWIN

Your chances of someone wanting to hack your business are 100%. Them gaining entry is largely dependent on you.

I live in rural Ohio, and even in these meandering and rolling hills laden with farmland and beautiful scenery, hackers exist. Cybercrime isn't just for big cities; it is a crime that is inclusive of each and every place in this world that has technology that is connected to the internet.

Basically, it can happen anywhere!

In larger urban areas, the internet is typically more reliable than it is in more rural locations. This means that it can be sporadic at times, which creates a different set of challenges for IT providers that are not used to these types of variations.

The single greatest disservice any business can do to their clients and to their livelihood is to believe that a breach will not happen to them. Odds are, it will. Over the past 45 days alone, I know of seven businesses that were compromised. And remember, I'm not in a large metropolitan area. Here's what's interesting about these 7 businesses that were invaded:

- 6 out of 7 of these breaches were because of a company employee error.
- 3 out of those 6 employees didn't realize what they'd done, and one actually denied it. ("No, it wasn't me! I swear.")

If you get attacked, you have to cast the blame game aside and get serious about what you're going to do. Because it is a serious problem. You need to focus on where to begin, and how to contain the risk as quickly as possible.

FORENSIC INVESTIGATIONS AND DATA RECOVERY PLANNING

Through a forensic investigation of your system(s), you can trace back to the device where the breach originated.

Janet was the billing clerk for the town's pediatrician and she checked her email quickly during her lunch break and saw a peculiar email from her best friend, Jessie. The subject line read: Check this out. There was a link with no message attached and Janet clicked on it, completely curious as to what it may be. It turned out to be nothing and the little circle just kept spinning (in "think" mode) and she clicked out of it and got back to work.

Well about 10 days later, Janet got to the office early one morning to get a head start on the billing from the previous day and she couldn't get logged into her accounting software; her email inbox wouldn't display...and then it happened—the big black screen and message: Your personal files have been locked.

It's at this point as an IT service provider that we usually get "the call." And yes, it's often frantic. Fast forward an hour and here is the assessment: no one can work, they can't login to their patient systems, they were unable to open Word or Excel documents, and they can't view any images. Everything is locked up. Backup was successful last night; but now it's GONE – deleted. File versions are locked up too.

The outbreaks continue as the month goes on. Sometimes it's just the "Microsoft" documents. Other victims include engineering files like AutoCAD and all the various drawing files. Sometimes just photos. It really depended on the business and what data they had.

Forensics for a hack is so important. You have to determine as quickly as possible:

- How the hacker intruded?
- How long they were there?
- What did they do while they were in the network?
- Did they still have a backdoor into the system?
- What did they take?

What came next was fast action for the IT Service Provider that included:

- Technology steps to halt any activity.
- Going into disaster recovery mode. Many of these offices had no plan, which made it more challenging than it should have been. A Disaster Recovery Plan (DRP) is the blueprint to recover.
- Determining if it made sense to contact the insurance company where the company has cyber liability insurance.
- Contacting the company attorney if Personally Identifiable Information (PII) had been exposed.
- The recognition that something had to be done to ensure the company protects their assets.

Situations like the aforementioned scenarios happen all the time and forensics is the master solver of the puzzle. When it comes to disaster recovery, none of these businesses had worked through the scenario, so recovery was a bigger challenge than it should have been. In talking with businesses, I often find that they have data all over the place. Imagine the anxiety of putting those pieces together in a hectic and stressful time?

SIX WAYS TO HELP AVOID A BREACH

You can never be 100% safe, but you can do many things to deter cybercriminals from wasting their time knocking on your business's door.

Any business that relies on technology in some manner (basically all) has daily risks involved in their line of work. This is why you need to focus on all the ways you can prevent a breach. Each one is a complement to the other. Together, they create a strong defense against a potential breach.

1. Have a firewall with security services

ACME Farm Supply purchased a router from Wal-Mart, believing it was a firewall that would protect them and their business's data. Imagine their surprise when they learned that it wasn't worth the plastic it was wrapped in. Hackers got into their system and spread a virus to their clients. The ease of set-up and the cost ended up costing them dearly.

A firewall isn't just purchased and installed. And it's not a "prevent all" on its own. The type of firewall that you want your business (regardless of size) to have will include a security service subscription.

Technology like this can provide unified threat management that stops unknown and zero day attacks at the entrance to your network. This service does not allow packets into the network until it can verify that they are a good, legitimate request.

Best yet, this filtering is done in real time and through the cloud so you are protecting yourself from today's threat, not yesterday's news. Threats change constantly and cybercriminals are always one step ahead of everyone else.

2. Purchase an antivirus subscription

The key to this is "purchase." Free antivirus subscriptions put you at the mercy of the vendor. They get around to performing security updates on their dime not yours. They have no obligation to you to remain current. Good services cost money; you want to be the customer not the product. You should demand assurances that:

- Your antivirus is being updated constantly. This service we offer through TTechT integrates with our dashboard so we get alerts with our remote managing tool.
- The antivirus is scanning. A docile antivirus is an ineffective antivirus, as it only takes a few seconds for a breach to detect an entry point into your system.
- Your choice antivirus provider has the latest definition files as soon as they are released. It's very important to have a service that is in constant communication with those who release these files.
- Although technology is amazing, with antivirus you must always have someone "watching" it. There is no better way to be proactive, and at TTechT, it is a 24/7 responsibility, not a Monday through Friday, 8-to-5 job.

3. Always perform patch updates promptly

We-C-U, Inc. is a growing and promising optometry business, and they are so lucky to have the owner's son's best friend agree to give them technological support at a bargain price. He promises to go into the business twice a month to perform updates. He goes in on the second Monday of the month, not realizing that many patch updates come out on the second Tuesday of every month (Microsoft). A week later, some bozo demanding ransom says that they needed five bitcoins to unlock all the files for We-C-U, Inc. In this case, the attacker did take files, but none contained PPI and all the backup and shadow copies were still available to restore.

What does this scenario teach us?

- Patch updates need immediate attention. The way you can best ensure this is to have a relationship with an IT provider. Trusting this "must-do" task to your employees or friends who have other responsibilities can cost you greatly.
- Even if you know when patches are typically released, when significant threats are revealed there can be patches that are released at other times. You must be ready!
- Every application a business uses will have patches (those updates that are available). Each patch needs individual attention and you should always demand assurances that they are being properly performed. Who is best equipped to give these important assurances? IT partners who can do these patch updates via a remote location work the best. Records of all work done can also be accessed for verification. Plus, the updates can interrupt productivity and temporarily disable a system so you should expect after-hours installation in order to maintain the best productivity.

4. Backup systems are essential

Sam purchased Million Dollar Seed from his father, who'd worked in the business for fifty years until he retired. The updates that his dad had been hesitant to do with their growing business were finally going to be done. Sam set a budget for next year. But it was this year that the server decided to crash. It was no problem, though, because they had tape backups (yes, they still exist). Imagine everyone's surprise when they found the tapes hadn't been working for what seemed like five years.

You can never have too many backup systems for your data, both on-site and off-site. The best backups are not visible to employees or those who may try to breach a system. They operate in the shadows – "shadow IT". This backup will reveal to business owners/managers where users have saved data and what they are using, and when. You can tell if they save to thumb drives and make sure you get copies of these things if they do.

Through all these efforts to have multiple backup systems, you can piece together a system crash or event and minimize the amount of data that has been lost. This is also a smart move because it's not a pleasant task to go to clients and tell them that you've lost all their data and information. Basically—you don't want your clients to be your backup source.

BONUS TIP: Mirroring your backup "drive" is dangerous, because if someone deletes the backup, the mirror will reflect the same, which is nothing. Mirrored backups equal zero saved data.

5. Only use email that has spam protection

Remember the information about what 6 out of 7 cyber breaches were, and Janet's story? Spam protection on her email would have prevented this, and while businesses can only protect their email addresses, they can make sure their employees don't fall victim to the scams that take place from suspicious emails. Here are a few points to remember:

- Internet Service Providers (ISP) hosted email is typically pop3 mail and this is not a secure connection.

An ISP's business is to provide you internet via their networking technology and equipment. Their forte is not to run an email server. By setting up your email with an SSL you will ensure that your messages cannot be read by an "internet sniffer".

- Pop email can be just like cookies and you can get targeted for spoof emails just like you get targeted for ads in your browsers.
- Be sure your administrator makes policies for email usage that are adhered to by all employees, such as strong passwords.
- Legitimate spam services will provide incoming and outgoing filtering.

6. Have employee training, follow-up, and accountability

It's been proven that busy employees with good intentions are the prime source of a breach. To lessen the risk, training is necessary and follow-up is critical. These are components that your business should have, and there are many ways to reinforce the message.

- Create consistent messaging for employees that offers reminders of "think before you click." If you become complacent, the best technology will not prevent an employee from performing an action they shouldn't. There is always someone trying to get into a system that shouldn't be there—be vigilant and alert.
- Have a formal training portal. TTechT has a portal that clients use to raise awareness of best practices for employees. This portal provides a one-stop-shop for policies and documentation, along with about 45-minutes of cyber security training, which includes a test at the end. We also offer weekly reminders of cyber safety tips and these are emailed to employees.
- Have signed employee policy agreements (Acceptable User Policy). These are the agreements in writing that show employees what is expected of them in regard

to using technology. This is important for businesses that have to follow compliance guidelines, and it also protects them better legally. They have sound recourse against a careless employee, should their actions lead to a breach. It eliminates the "I didn't know."

• Have an annual cyber-safety review.

When you are busy creating a living and you feel invincible because you haven't fallen victim to a cybercrime yet, it's easy to put security and prevention aside for another day. But ask yourself, can you guarantee that you'll get to it before the attack reaches you?

When it comes to your security systems and the protective measures you have in place to protect your data and company reputation, be proactive in finding a solution. Tomorrow's Technology Today, LLC always welcomes these conversations because they are so important. Don't wait to have the talk that will give you real information about your levels of protection and security solutions.

About Lisa

With over 20 years of technology and business experience, Lisa Niekamp-Urwin is President and CEO of Tomorrow's Technology Today in St. Henry, Ohio. Founded in 2002, Tomorrow's Technology Today (TTechT) is a technology service provider for rural Ohio. Lisa attended the University of Dayton for Computer Science and then the University of Findlay for Business Management. She also holds a Project Management Professional accreditation from the Project Management Institute, along with a Master's from George Washington University in Project Management. Lisa founded TTechT on the passion and love of technology, and in the excitement to bring enterprise technology to the small and medium-size businesses in the area.

Lisa has developed a unique cyber-security service for businesses in rural Ohio and beyond. Cyber security means layers of protection and implementing an enterprise level solution that performs at industry standards without breaking the bank account. This includes firewalls, backup with disaster recovery ability, business class antivirus, patch management, email with enterprise level protection services, and employee education.

Lisa is married to Frank and has two beautiful daughters, Brittany and Brianne. She grew up showing horses and has given this passion to their girls. When time permits, the girls "let" Mom show their horse also. The three, and sometimes Frank too, travel throughout the Midwest to show at the national level AQHA horse shows. Beyond technology and horses, Lisa also enjoys watching her daughters in ballet productions and gymnastics competitions.

Lisa says: "I love this business and the opportunities and friends it has brought to my life. I wouldn't trade this for the world and I hope it shows in the way we do business. We love what we do! Of course some days bring us great challenges and other days bring us great rewards, but that is technology!"

CHAPTER 15

SECURE YOUR BUSINESS BY SECURING YOUR DATA

BY JOEL GULICK
– President and CEO of Computer Solutions, Inc.

It doesn't matter what your business is;
somebody is going to be interested in your data.

A costly mistake businesses can make is to assume that their technology-stored data is not important—or of interest to someone else. Nothing could be further from the truth, whether you are a smaller retail-based industry or a health-related business that works with primary care. Let's face it, that data and information you have on your customers means a great deal to how you run your business. You can't just ask a client to resubmit their private information or retake that x-ray if you lose what they've already offered. On the other hand, devious outside parties and/ or employees can think of plenty of reasons why they would love to have access to what you have, either stealing it from you or making you go through various obstacles to retrieve it.

Does your business use or rely on any of this information?

- Personally Identifiable Information (PII): this is an extensive list that includes names, addresses, birthdates, social security

numbers, telephone numbers, employment information, insurance information, credit card information, etc.
- Intellectual property: this is inclusive of anything creative that belongs to you or your business, and is meant for use for your business's platform and profitability. Patents, copyrights, and trademarks fall under this category.
- Client data that you use to operate your business: this would be any and all lists and information on clients that an employee could take with them if they left, possibly costing you business and credibility.

As you can see, a computer system can hold just about everything a business requires to run operations effectively. Having a record of all the information is an important part of protecting a business and maintaining its integrity.

A strong focus on customer service is no excuse for a lack of effort in securing the data that you require to effectively run your business.

You want to take care of your customers, and we get that. This is why the safeguards that you can put in place via technology are so important. You need to know which known and unknown parties are accessing or trying to access your data. If something were to happen where someone who shouldn't have your data takes it and runs with it, there are two things that a sound back-up system offers:

1. The ability to restore the data.
2. Reports to show you exactly where your data was compromised, and if it was done externally, by whom.

For medical-based industries and financial industries, properly-executed data backup is a requirement of compliance, and a necessary focus in successful business practices. For non-related medical businesses, it does offer customers assurances that you take the data they give you seriously. If you want an example of when things go wrong, you don't need to look further than the news and all the stories about data breaches that have taken place.

SEVEN BENEFITS OF DATA BACKUP

If you were to find yourself in a data crisis, for any reason, how much data could you afford to lose and still remain in business?

If you are a business owner or in a leadership role, you need to embrace the importance of data protection in your company. There is no exception to this rule. Because if you don't, it will go noticed and you might find yourself playing clean-up from one of the following scenarios:

- A disgruntled employee sabotaging or stealing your data (which can be a slow trick theft, taking place over several years' worth of time, even).
- A known or unknown entity creating problems with your data, either by falsifying it or releasing it to the "highest bidder." All data is of interest to a cybercriminal, either in hopes of receiving a ransom payment for it (they encrypt it until you pay) or by selling what they gain access to on the black web (a hotspot for theft).

These things will take place if you do not take action. With the right planning and policies in place and through having data backed up in a manner that gives the utmost protection to your business and your clients, you give yourself more security, more protection.

1. **Data integrity on backups:**
   By securing backup, you can prevent dangerous people from changing your backups. For example, you have companies small and large with data bases, law firms have legal documentation, medical firms have tests, and in the medical field you cannot charge again for what you've lost through a lack of policies and procedures against crime. Then there is ransomware—if your data becomes encrypted your business

will be shut down until you pay. Paying a criminal for your information is a bothersome thought from most accounts. And there are no assurances that they won't take the money and information and run. What makes ransomware even scarier is that most companies will go out of business if they don't pay it. Yet, when you pay it, you're making yourself a bigger target. The solution is to avoid it through secure backup systems!

2. Proper employee security procedures:

With backups, if you don't have a secure set-up against threats, you are really not backing up your data. You're just buying time before something happens and real damage takes place. Attacks can happen in many forms. Consider the CEO who is about to get fired and knows it. How do you handle this situation so you can protect your data and deter any theft or malicious intent? The solution is to lock everything out prior to their dismissal so you can protect all outgoing emails (in case they transfer data to their personal email) and stop all attachments from going through. It's disheartening to have to acknowledge that people are willing to be more devious today because of technology, yet it is necessary.

An effective solution is to not give all people access to all parts of the system. Even upper management can just access what is necessary for their specific job functions, even if they feel that they should be able to access everything. It's a simple step that helps alleviate the temptations that may unknowingly exist to you, the business owner.

3. Time stamps are a part of good backup systems:

Time stamps show when information is accessed, transferred, or manipulated in some way. There is no better way to know who was looking at what information, and when. With time stamps, the clues that reveal both employee and hacker behaviors can be uncovered. However, this is most likely to happen when you have a vested partnership with an IT provider that understands what to look for, and has systems in place that are working for you, even when you're technically not working.

4. Single-Use passwords:

To control how often certain data is accessed, you can create systems that have "one time use" passwords. This means that a password is no longer valid after it's been used to access information one time. This is a highly effective way to ensure that you know exactly who is looking at your company's most protected data and when. It's a very hands-on approach, but depending on the type of information your business accesses (for example, highly classified or intellectual property), you are more alert to who's viewing your property and when.

5. Prevention of espionage and embezzlement:

The world of cybercrime is a high-tech world, and despite what you may wish to believe, these criminals are not afraid to look you right in the eye as they plan out their crime. There is a risk of someone coming to work for you from a competitor just to learn what you have going on and report back to their "old employer." Or to use it for their own personal gain in some manner. By taking steps to have a proper data backup in place, you can create a more relaxing and engaging work environment that doesn't feel paranoid or suspicious. It's a smart move!

6. Stopping loss of business data:

The hackers who are trying to get into your system work nonstop. They have software in place that knows where to look on your cyber-blueprint for your open door so they can enter into your system and begin to steal, manipulate, or compromise your data. When you combine bugs created by software and the high risk of human error (due to improper training), you should be compelled to take actions that help your business not lose any more data than absolutely necessary. If you pass on this action, it can become a costly mistake. Imagine if you owned a nuclear facility and someone who had bad intentions gained access to those codes. That would be a serious crisis, wouldn't it? Your business may not be "nuclear", but if it deals with data, you are likely subject to penalties and fines, could lose your hard-earned good reputation overnight, and may also face legal consequences which can result in a "closed" sign on your door.

7. If all else fails, remember your data equals cash to a criminal:
Any of your business data that a criminal can get his or her hands on, is considered a paycheck to them. They can use it themselves or sell it to someone else who knows just what to do with it. And if you can count on anything, you can count on the fact that they are not looking out for your best interests when they do so.

THREE WAYS TO ENSURE YOU ARE USING BEST PRACTICES FOR DATA BACKUP

Data backup empowers business and can lock the door against hackers and disgruntled employees.

We'll never be able to be 100% safe from our business being sabotaged through another party's malicious intentions. Thankfully, engaging in an IT partnership can help you understand your best options. You have to understand what you have, and know that it is offering the protections you believe it is.

1. Don't assume your cybersecurity is covered by anyone's insurance:
IT providers should have E&O insurance, but don't assume that it will cover you if something goes wrong. Likewise, don't assume your business's E&O insurance is going to cover a potential breach in your security. Make sure you

have a thoughtful conversation with your IT provider, as well as with your business insurance agent that gives you insight into how you are currently protected if there was a breach, or even an equipment malfunction. Find out about cyber insurance from a qualified representative, as well.

2. Have a contract with a reputable IT service provider:

Not every IT provider offers the same services or has the same level of expertise. Part of our guiding principles at Computer Solutions, Inc. is to ensure that:

- We have a plan in place for unexpected issues.
- We give protection to your data network and systems to alert us to potential hackings and virus threats—and then stop them from being successful in their pursuit of your system.
- We have effective recovery plans where you will be able to restore your data and system promptly if it's ever compromised.

3. Training on ways to use your technology to prevent theft:

Cameras and monitors are excellent resources for finding the habits and patterns of potential criminals that want what you have. Unfortunately, many businesses never review footage until they realize they have a theft. Notice it's "realize." You're busy and have a lot to do, which is why we have the ability to look for activities both via camera footage and digital blueprints in your system. Slow trickles of theft from a business are not uncommon, and having a strategy to pay better attention to what your cameras and technology tell you about activity makes a difference in your profit margin and stifling criminal behavior. The evidence is often in the backup.

LEARNING TO OUTSMART THE CRIMINALS

The easiest way to keep a person honest is to put a lock on the door. This is exactly what the right technology infrastructure can do for you.

The last thing we want is for businesses to be afraid to be innovative and grow. It's much more exciting to focus on creating work cultures that are product-, service-, and consumer-driven. Yet, there is an obligation to go about this in a smart way.

It's easy to focus on what your business is good at and what you're passionate about, which is why you need to seek out people who are passionate about technology to make sure you are protected.

Admittedly, cybercriminals still have an edge in the game of theft. This is mostly because they exploit patches and fixes to technology before they can be corrected. There are IT businesses today that are helping to stop these cybercriminals in their tracks by studying their habits and patterns before they infiltrate a system. It's a smart move and one that it important in determining effective, functional client strategies from our perspective at Computer Solutions, Inc.

Success leaves clues, it's not reinventing the wheel. Thankfully, this is a two-way street: one way has the cybercriminals trying to get into the fast lane of your internet, and the other way has you, the business, setting up the barriers that stop them from going fast. In fact, you can reroute them and deter them from even considering you for their deviant acts.

In a world where there is so much opportunity for criminals, having secure data backup and policies in place is a safeguard that will encourage unsavory parties to move on. Why waste time on your business when it's easy to find another one that isn't prepared and has left their door open?

About Joel

Joel Gulick is author of *Getting I.T. Right!* and president of Computer Solutions Inc., a Managed Service Provider located in Savannah, Georgia. What started as fixing the family computer's motherboard as a teenager, bloomed into a love for technology, and in turn, turned into one of Savannah's leading IT Companies. Founded in 2005, Computer Solutions Inc., has focused on helping business owners particularly in the medical industry, maintain and grow their operations through efficient technology uses, industry best practices, practical resource utilization and custom software applications. Joel's 'can-do' attitude and 'work-smarter-not-harder' approach has made him a well-respected professional in the industry. With an understanding of psychology and a sound ability to analyze problems and efficiently implement solutions, give him an edge above the rest.

Joel's "glass is half-full mentality" has allowed him to break through some of the most challenging barriers and help fellow business owners do the same. He focuses on helping businesses with their technology needs, as well as helping them to be as efficient as possible in their specialized areas of service. With a variety of custom solutions, streamlined processes and procedures, Joel enables businesses to focus on their productivity without unnecessary IT headaches and associated downtime.

When he's not working, Joel enjoys spending time with his family and a variety of outdoor activities, such as being out on the water or at the beach, skiing, water sports, traveling to new places, music festivals, and good food.

Joel's driving motto is, "Success leaves clues." He states, "...that too often, people are reinventing the wheel instead of taking what works and developing from there."

Find Joel at:
- https://www.linkedin.com/in/joel-gulick
- www.computerserviceandrepair.com I 912.921.7889
- www.facebook.com/savannahitshop

CHAPTER 16

HOW TO CONTROL AND SECURE BYOD DEMAND

BY CHRIS H. DAVENPORT
– Co-founder of 3i International

With the introduction of Bring Your Own Device (BYOD) to work, the way business is conducted has taken a drastic shift.

In order for businesses to remain competitive, many are being forced to consider implementing BYOD for their organization. The benefits are numerous, which makes it an appealing option to consider.

- Users (employees) can work from home just as easily as the office.
- Users are more productive.
- Employees are able to use their preferred device, as they are the ones who purchase it.

Basically, equipping employees with the ability to access their work from anywhere allows them to do more with their time. There are fewer restrictions. This sounds great, right? It is, but you also have to understand what the risks are. After all, BYOD is not exempt from compliance issues that may be standard in your industry.

Without the proper policies and procedures in place what seems like a good idea for productivity can have the exact opposite effect. It can turn a business on its ear, creating tough challenges that are expensive (both in cost and reputation) to rebound from. As a business decision maker, you never want your story of a cyber-breach on your organization to become "the story" of the day in your community, or even on a national or international level.

WHEN A BREACH SNEAKS IN

*If there is a way to enter into your network,
a malware or ransomware virus will find it.*

No business or individual ever desires for a virus to infiltrate their computer, smart phone, tablet, etc. The creators of malware and ransomware are intelligent and clever individuals, knowing that if they are persistent they will find a device that isn't prepared to defend against their attack. Then they will enter into a computer through this "back door" and find their way into all technology that's linked to that system. This is the reality of how this works; viruses are like a fast-rooting plant that spreads and grows rapidly.

We recently had a customer that was using BYOD and an employee had brought a device in from their home and was allowed to connect to the business network with it. All was well and the device was being used on-site for weeks. No problems were detected, which meant that no one realized there was malware on the device and it had worked its way into the business's entire network.

As the employee worked from their device, the malware was spreading everywhere and even onto other peoples' devices. It was collecting information and learning and waiting for the right time to have its perpetrator act.

This was a real threat that remained undetected by everyone. The first viruses created were meant to disrupt and annoy, but today's viruses don't come with animated characters and blinking lights. They work quietly, alerting no one to their presence.

This malware eventually lead to a connection with an offshore network that was on the internet. It allowed a keylogger to occur on a few of the PCs at the business. Through these logs collected, they were able to determine how the process for requesting wire transfers took place.

The hackers gained access to a great deal of information, including the protocol, the person(s) who authorized wire transfers, and exactly how an email would look that authorized a funds transfer. Then good fortune set in, as they had also learned the CFO who handled those functions was going on vacation.

Here's what the hackers did next:

1. They sent out an email that looked like it was from the CFO—just one letter off—and it said that when they were gone there was one important wire transfer that would have to take place, and they shared the pertinent information about that transfer.
2. The email that requested the transfer was sent to the person in charge of wires in the CFO's absence. It was a request for a transfer of $345,000.00.

Imagine the CFO's surprise to come back from vacation and learn that they authorized that wire transfer. No, they had not. The hackers were already long gone and a whole lot richer from their scheme.

We were called in and were able to do forensics and trace back to the source where the attack started—it was the device that an employee had brought in from home. After that, we got to work setting up the policies and procedures that would prevent this business from participating in risky BYOD practices and get their systems up-to-speed on the better way to do BYOD.

Can you see why BYOD is important to properly manage? You never want to be the business that ends up having 345,000 reasons why it "would" have been good to take the right steps "before" the breach happened.

THE SIX PARTS OF SECURING BYOD FOR YOUR WORKPLACE

BYOD security is inclusive of 6 parts. You cannot expect the protection your business needs if you don't properly address all the parts, and also incorporate the proper training on why they are necessary—not optional.

The errors of not having a fully encompassing BYOD policy in place can be costly enough that they impact your business permanently. It's always exciting to see businesses being proactive to ensure they are doing what's right for BYOD policy, rather than scrambling after a cyber-event unfolds. 3i International has made it our obligation to inform and assist businesses with BYOD. It's a growing way to do business, and also a rising trend. Still, if you are going to do it, you had best make sure you do it the right way—right away.

1. **Separate your BYOD Wi-Fi network on a separate VLAN (Virtual Local Area Network):**
   Most businesses have one Wi-Fi connection for all aspects of their business. When you decide to implement BYOD you will need to adjust this. The way you do this is by establishing a VLAN. The benefits of this separate network include:

   - More stringent rules
   - It's segregated off from other corporate networks and VLANs, on an island of its own, so to speak

   By having a network that only gets internet access at a VLAN point, BYOD users won't be allowed directly into the corporate network. This helps to isolate a hack or malicious link, which is what criminals cast out there, but you can prevent from impacting you. The policies that go along with this are such that if there was to be ransomware detected, an alert would immediately go to the administrator and that device would be shunned from accessing the network. If the threat spreads, it is also easier to isolate and manage it.

2. Have a secure gateway with threat protection:

This is a device that you have at the internet connection point in your business. The secure gateway allows you to set up a separate Wi-Fi network on one of the entry points of your network. Within the gateway, you can treat the network much like it was an "untrusted network." This means that you are able to set stringent rules that will not allow that device to access the corporate network. As the IT partner, we are able to help monitor and pinpoint threats on any devices to make sure they are safe and if there are any caution signs, we make sure they cannot access the network.

3. Client VPN:

You've created a set Wi-Fi and gateway, which means that it is also time to set up a client VPN. What this does is allow someone access to corporate resources with their device after it has gone through a secure gateway that has not detected any malware. Basically, the device has been vetted, and then the VPN is in place to give the access. This is controlled in a way that you can apply more policies to it, which help to prevent data from being misused. Additionally, this offers another way to layer authentication to ensure the right people are on the system, and it also requires that you have a valid business account to gain access.

4. Mobile Device Management (MDM) for email and app provisioning:

MDM is the solution that allows you to disable other Wi-Fi networks when someone is in the business one. With this, we can also publish applications that are centric to business functions that are internal and push the email out. The good thing about this is that you are able to control the security settings on devices so you can do things such as:

- Require pin codes so devices cannot remain open when not in use
- Require the minimum versions of certain applications that are acceptable to use
- Have a list of devices that are no longer supported by updates and limit what those devices have access to
- Wipe corporate data from lost or stolen devices
- Wipe corporate data from the devices of employees that are fired or resign from the organization

MDM is also what is necessary to help ensure you are not breaking the law by comingling company and personal data together. It allows employees personal data—such as passwords, social media, etc., to remain private, while isolating the data, apps, and resources to do their work functions on that device.

5. **Leverage RemoteApp to keep corporate data off the device:**

RemoteApp is a Microsoft product which is based on the remote desktop protocol, and allows publishing applications that would normally run on a desktop computer. Because of this, the types of applications you can publish are limitless. It gives the security and compatibility to allow you to run these apps on personal devices such as iPads and tablets. With this product, you are able see the application layer appear on the screen, but no data actually goes onto the device. This helps give you control and therefore you can better maintain the integrity of corporate data while allowing end users access to do their work.

You can also set up provisions regarding which functions you will, or will not, allow to happen. For example, you can make it so: a) external drives cannot be used, and b) redirecting to various other storage devices is not allowed.

Additionally, an audit trail feature is available where you can keep track of everything that takes place on devices related to your business. You can know who accesses what information, and when. This feature also allows you to set time limitations so if you don't want to grant access to information after business hours, you can set those parameters.

6. Implement an Acceptable Use Policy (AUP) for the network:

A lot of initial consultations that we have uncover a large concern—many businesses have failed to implement an AUP. Some may feel they have this policy in place, but it doesn't fully cover them when it comes to BYOD concerns. This is important for many reasons:

- The AUP is a safeguard for your company.
- This policy is what will lay out the recourse for employees who do not follow the procedures you've put in place for safe BYOD.
- It sets a clear precedent for your HR department.
- By having an AUP, you are setting a clear expectation of both BYOD policies and network policies that help to bring awareness to employees about better practices for business, and actually their personal lives, as well.
- The policy is actually a reminder, and training manual of what employees should do to make safer choices with technology every time they touch it. The habits that come with practicing good user policies will become habit.

Controlled and secure BYOD is not just a hope, it's an expectation. The businesses who are committed to implementing the necessary steps to embrace this growing "way to work" will find themselves at an advantage. They'll have more highly productive employees, and fewer risks of hacks that can sabotage their business.

WHAT COMES NEXT?

Whether you currently have BYOD or you're considering it, it's time to have a meaningful assessment of your options.

The ultimate goal of a good BYOD rollout will allow your employees to get their work done on the devices of their choice— all with the least amount of hassles and challenges. This can lead to stellar results for your business, as well as your employees overall job satisfaction.

It is impossible to have safe and reliable BYOD for your business if you don't invest in the proper components to ensure its reliability. It's supposed to work for you, not against you, at all times. At 3i International, we bring a thoughtful and thorough discussion to the table that explains the way a proper BYOD implementation works and how to put it into place. These are things that cannot be left to chance.

With every part in place, your BYOD policy is valuable, and will make you less vulnerable.

About Chris

Chris H. Davenport has made a career putting his expertise to work for some of the world's leading brands, delivering a level of skill and support that has made him the "go-to" guy for companies that need IT issues addressed fast and effectively.

He has worked with high-visibility global clients like Yahoo and Bank of America, providing a range of capabilities that includes a deep knowledge of hardware and software, server security, network performance, and systems and technology integration. During his 20 years as an Information Technology professional, he has served as a consultant and hands-on solutions provider, either complementing and supporting a client's existing technology team, or functioning as an in-house manager of IT.

As a reflection of his unique talents, Chris has become known by the nicknames, "The Cleaner" or "The Wolf," a nod to the character in the film *Pulp Fiction* who was cool under pressure and could solve problems that were seemingly without solutions.